# 50 New York City Food Recipes for Home

By: Kelly Johnson

# Table of Contents

- New York-style Bagels
- Classic NYC Pizza
- Pastrami on Rye
- New York Cheesecake
- Black and White Cookies
- Egg Cream
- Manhattan Clam Chowder
- New York-style Hot Dogs
- Chicken and Rice from the Halal Cart
- Corned Beef Hash
- New York-style Knish
- Spicy Sausage and Pepper Hero
- Classic Reuben Sandwich
- NYC Pretzels
- Lobster Roll
- New York-style Bialys
- Cheesesteak
- Creamy New York-style Rice Pudding
- New York-style Roast Beef Sandwich
- Garlic Knots
- Brooklyn-style Pizza
- Lemon Ricotta Pancakes
- Eggplant Parmesan Hero
- NYC Deli Pickles
- Sweet and Sour Cabbage Soup
- New York-style Buffalo Wings
- Pork Belly Bao Buns
- Beef Stroganoff
- Lobster Mac and Cheese
- NYC-style Chicken Parmesan
- Cinnamon Sugar Donuts
- Classic NY Style Eggplant Rollatini
- Stuffed Artichokes
- Pastry Cream-filled Eclairs
- Hot Pastrami on Rye
- New York-style Frittata

- Shrimp Scampi
- Classic NYC Meatballs
- Fresh Ricotta with Honey
- New York-style Potato Latkes
- Coney Island Hot Dogs
- New York-style Beef Brisket
- Blackened Salmon
- Classic NYC Meatloaf
- Bagel with Lox and Cream Cheese
- Sweet and Sour Meatballs
- Roasted Garlic Mashed Potatoes
- Classic NYC Chicken Soup
- NYC-style Chopped Cheese
- New York-style Apple Pie

**New York-style Bagels**

**Ingredients:**

- **For the Dough:**
    - 4 cups all-purpose flour
    - 1 tablespoon granulated sugar
    - 1 tablespoon active dry yeast (or 2 1/4 teaspoons instant yeast)
    - 1 1/2 cups warm water (110°F to 115°F / 45°C)
    - 1 1/2 teaspoons salt
- **For Boiling:**
    - 2 quarts (2 liters) water
    - 2 tablespoons granulated sugar
    - 1 tablespoon baking soda
- **For Topping:**
    - 1 egg, beaten (for egg wash)
    - Sesame seeds, poppy seeds, or coarse sea salt (optional)

**Instructions:**

1. **Prepare the Dough:**
    - In a small bowl, dissolve the sugar in warm water and sprinkle the yeast on top. Let it sit for 5-10 minutes until frothy.
    - In a large mixing bowl, combine the flour and salt.
    - Make a well in the center and pour in the yeast mixture. Stir until a dough forms.
    - Turn the dough out onto a lightly floured surface and knead for about 10 minutes until smooth and elastic. You can also use a stand mixer with a dough hook for this step.
2. **First Rise:**
    - Place the dough in a lightly oiled bowl, cover it with a clean cloth or plastic wrap, and let it rise in a warm place for about 1 hour, or until doubled in size.
3. **Shape the Bagels:**
    - Punch down the dough and turn it out onto a lightly floured surface.
    - Divide the dough into 12 equal pieces and shape each piece into a ball.
    - To shape the bagels, poke a hole through the center of each ball with your finger, then gently stretch the hole to about 1-2 inches in diameter.
4. **Second Rise:**
    - Place the shaped bagels on a parchment-lined baking sheet or a lightly floured surface. Cover with a cloth and let rise for 30 minutes.
5. **Preheat Oven:**
    - Preheat your oven to 425°F (220°C).
6. **Boil the Bagels:**
    - In a large pot, bring the water to a boil and add the sugar and baking soda.

- Gently drop the bagels into the boiling water, a few at a time, and boil for about 1 minute per side. Use a slotted spoon to remove them and place them back on the parchment-lined baking sheet.
7. **Add Toppings:**
    - Brush the tops of the bagels with the beaten egg.
    - Sprinkle with sesame seeds, poppy seeds, or coarse sea salt if desired.
8. **Bake:**
    - Bake the bagels in the preheated oven for 20-25 minutes, or until golden brown and crisp on the outside.
9. **Cool:**
    - Allow the bagels to cool on a wire rack before slicing and enjoying.

These New York-style bagels are perfect with cream cheese, lox, or your favorite spreads. Enjoy your homemade bagels!

**Classic NYC Pizza**

**Ingredients:**

- **For the Dough:**
    - 2 1/4 teaspoons (1 packet) active dry yeast
    - 1 1/2 cups warm water (110°F to 115°F / 45°C)
    - 4 cups all-purpose flour
    - 1 1/2 teaspoons salt
    - 1 tablespoon olive oil
    - 1 tablespoon granulated sugar
- **For the Sauce:**
    - 1 can (15 ounces) tomato sauce
    - 1 can (6 ounces) tomato paste
    - 2 cloves garlic, minced
    - 1 teaspoon dried oregano
    - 1 teaspoon dried basil
    - 1/2 teaspoon sugar
    - Salt and black pepper to taste
- **For the Topping:**
    - 2 cups shredded mozzarella cheese
    - 1/2 cup grated Parmesan cheese
    - 1/2 cup sliced pepperoni (optional)
    - Fresh basil leaves for garnish (optional)
    - Red pepper flakes (optional)

**Instructions:**

1. **Prepare the Dough:**
    - In a small bowl, dissolve the sugar in the warm water and sprinkle the yeast on top. Let it sit for 5-10 minutes until frothy.
    - In a large bowl, combine the flour and salt.
    - Make a well in the center and pour in the yeast mixture and olive oil. Stir until a dough forms.
    - Turn the dough out onto a lightly floured surface and knead for about 7-10 minutes until smooth and elastic. You can also use a stand mixer with a dough hook for this step.
2. **First Rise:**
    - Place the dough in a lightly oiled bowl, cover it with a cloth or plastic wrap, and let it rise in a warm place for about 1-2 hours, or until doubled in size.
3. **Prepare the Sauce:**
    - In a medium bowl, combine the tomato sauce, tomato paste, minced garlic, oregano, basil, sugar, salt, and pepper. Mix well and set aside.
4. **Preheat Oven:**

- Preheat your oven to 500°F (260°C). If you have a pizza stone, place it in the oven while it preheats.

5. **Shape the Dough:**
    - Punch down the dough and turn it out onto a lightly floured surface.
    - Divide the dough in half for two medium pizzas or keep it whole for one large pizza.
    - Roll out or stretch the dough into a thin circle or rectangle, depending on your preference and baking surface.

6. **Assemble the Pizza:**
    - Transfer the rolled-out dough to a lightly floured pizza peel or a parchment-lined baking sheet.
    - Spread a thin layer of pizza sauce over the dough, leaving a small border around the edges.
    - Sprinkle the shredded mozzarella cheese evenly over the sauce.
    - Add the grated Parmesan cheese and any additional toppings like pepperoni if desired.

7. **Bake:**
    - Slide the pizza onto the preheated pizza stone (or place the baking sheet in the oven).
    - Bake for 10-15 minutes, or until the crust is golden and the cheese is bubbly and slightly browned.

8. **Finish and Serve:**
    - Remove the pizza from the oven and let it cool slightly before slicing.
    - Garnish with fresh basil leaves and red pepper flakes if desired.

Enjoy your classic NYC pizza with its crispy crust, gooey cheese, and delicious toppings!

**Pastrami on Rye**

**Ingredients:**

- **For the Sandwich:**
    - 8 slices rye bread
    - 1 pound (450 grams) pastrami, sliced
    - 1/4 cup yellow mustard (or more, to taste)
    - Pickles, for serving (optional)
- **For the Mustard Spread (Optional):**
    - 1/4 cup Dijon mustard
    - 2 tablespoons honey
    - 1 tablespoon prepared horseradish

**Instructions:**

1. **Prepare the Pastrami:**
    - If the pastrami is not pre-sliced, slice it thinly against the grain. You can also warm the pastrami slightly if you prefer it hot. To do this, place it in a skillet over medium heat, stirring occasionally until heated through.
2. **Prepare the Mustard Spread (Optional):**
    - In a small bowl, combine the Dijon mustard, honey, and prepared horseradish. Mix until well combined. Adjust the ingredients to taste if desired.
3. **Assemble the Sandwich:**
    - Spread a layer of yellow mustard (or the mustard spread if using) on one side of each slice of rye bread.
    - Pile the warmed pastrami evenly on half of the bread slices.
    - Top with the remaining bread slices to form sandwiches.
4. **Serve:**
    - Serve the sandwiches with pickles on the side if desired.

This Pastrami on Rye is simple but incredibly satisfying, with the rich flavor of pastrami perfectly complemented by the tangy mustard and the hearty rye bread. Enjoy!

**New York Cheesecake**

**Ingredients:**

- **For the Crust:**
    - 1 1/2 cups graham cracker crumbs (about 10-12 graham crackers)
    - 1/4 cup granulated sugar
    - 1/2 cup unsalted butter, melted
- **For the Filling:**
    - 4 (8-ounce) packages cream cheese, softened
    - 1 cup granulated sugar
    - 1 teaspoon vanilla extract
    - 4 large eggs
    - 1 cup sour cream
    - 1 cup heavy cream
- **For the Topping (Optional):**
    - Fresh fruit (e.g., strawberries, blueberries) or fruit sauce
    - Whipped cream

**Instructions:**

1. **Prepare the Crust:**
    - Preheat your oven to 325°F (163°C).
    - In a medium bowl, combine the graham cracker crumbs, sugar, and melted butter. Mix until the crumbs are well coated and the mixture resembles wet sand.
    - Press the crumb mixture evenly into the bottom of a 9-inch springform pan to form the crust. Use the back of a spoon or a flat-bottomed glass to press it down firmly.
    - Bake the crust in the preheated oven for 10 minutes. Remove from the oven and set aside to cool.
2. **Prepare the Filling:**
    - In a large mixing bowl, beat the cream cheese until smooth and creamy.
    - Gradually add the sugar, beating until combined.
    - Mix in the vanilla extract.
    - Add the eggs one at a time, beating on low speed after each addition until just combined. Be careful not to overmix.
    - Gently fold in the sour cream and heavy cream until smooth.
3. **Bake the Cheesecake:**
    - Pour the cream cheese filling over the pre-baked crust in the springform pan.
    - Smooth the top with a spatula.
    - To prevent cracks, you can bake the cheesecake using a water bath. To do this, wrap the outside of the springform pan with aluminum foil to prevent leaks. Place the pan in a larger roasting pan and fill the roasting pan with hot water until it reaches halfway up the sides of the springform pan.

- Bake in the preheated oven for 1 hour and 10 minutes, or until the edges are set and the center is slightly jiggly. The cheesecake will continue to set as it cools.

4. **Cool and Chill:**
    - Turn off the oven and crack the oven door slightly. Let the cheesecake cool in the oven for 1 hour.
    - Remove the cheesecake from the oven and the water bath, and let it cool to room temperature.
    - Refrigerate the cheesecake for at least 4 hours, preferably overnight, to fully set and develop flavor.
5. **Serve:**
    - Before serving, you can top the cheesecake with fresh fruit or a fruit sauce if desired.
    - Optionally, add a dollop of whipped cream.

Enjoy your rich and creamy New York Cheesecake with its classic graham cracker crust and deliciously smooth filling!

**Black and White Cookies**

**Ingredients:**

- **For the Cookies:**
    - 2 1/2 cups all-purpose flour
    - 1 teaspoon baking powder
    - 1/2 teaspoon salt
    - 1/2 cup unsalted butter, softened
    - 1 cup granulated sugar
    - 2 large eggs
    - 1 cup buttermilk
    - 1 teaspoon vanilla extract
- **For the Icing:**
    - 1 cup powdered sugar
    - 1 tablespoon light corn syrup
    - 1/2 teaspoon vanilla extract
    - 2-3 tablespoons water
    - 1/2 cup powdered sugar (for the chocolate icing)
    - 1 tablespoon unsweetened cocoa powder
    - 1/2 tablespoon light corn syrup
    - 1-2 tablespoons water

**Instructions:**

1. **Prepare the Cookies:**
    - Preheat your oven to 350°F (175°C). Line a baking sheet with parchment paper.
    - In a medium bowl, whisk together the flour, baking powder, and salt.
    - In a large bowl, cream the butter and sugar together until light and fluffy.
    - Add the eggs one at a time, beating well after each addition.
    - Mix in the vanilla extract.
    - Gradually add the dry ingredients to the butter mixture, alternating with the buttermilk, beginning and ending with the dry ingredients. Mix until just combined.
    - Drop rounded tablespoons of dough onto the prepared baking sheet, spacing them about 2 inches apart.
    - Bake for 12-15 minutes, or until the edges are lightly golden. Cool on a wire rack.
2. **Prepare the Icing:**
    - **For the Vanilla Icing:**
        - In a medium bowl, whisk together 1 cup powdered sugar, corn syrup, vanilla extract, and enough water to achieve a spreadable consistency (about 2-3 tablespoons). The icing should be thick but spreadable.
    - **For the Chocolate Icing:**
        - In a small bowl, sift together 1/2 cup powdered sugar and cocoa powder.

- Mix in the corn syrup and enough water (about 1-2 tablespoons) to achieve a spreadable consistency. Adjust the amount of water to get the right consistency.
3. **Ice the Cookies:**
    - Once the cookies are completely cooled, spread the vanilla icing over half of each cookie.
    - Let the vanilla icing set for about 10-15 minutes.
    - Spread the chocolate icing over the other half of each cookie.
    - Allow the icing to set completely before serving.

These Black and White Cookies are perfect with a cup of coffee or tea and offer a delightful combination of flavors and textures. Enjoy your classic New York treat!

**Egg Cream**

**Ingredients:**

- 1/4 cup chocolate syrup (preferably Fox's U-Bet for an authentic taste)
- 1 cup cold milk (whole milk is preferred)
- 1 cup seltzer or carbonated water (chilled)

**Instructions:**

1. **Combine the Chocolate Syrup and Milk:**
    - In a tall glass, pour in the chocolate syrup.
    - Add the cold milk and stir until the syrup is fully incorporated with the milk.
2. **Add the Seltzer:**
    - Slowly pour the chilled seltzer into the glass, pouring gently to prevent excessive fizzing.
    - Stir lightly to combine, making sure not to overmix to preserve the frothy texture.
3. **Serve:**
    - Enjoy immediately with a straw. The egg cream should have a frothy, creamy head on top.

The Egg Cream is a simple but beloved New York classic, offering a sweet and fizzy treat that brings back memories of old-school soda fountains.

## Manhattan Clam Chowder

**Ingredients:**

- 4 slices bacon, chopped
- 1 large onion, finely chopped
- 2 cloves garlic, minced
- 2 celery stalks, chopped
- 1 bell pepper (red or green), chopped
- 2 medium carrots, diced
- 1 can (14.5 ounces) diced tomatoes, with juice
- 1 can (6 ounces) tomato paste
- 4 cups clam juice or seafood stock
- 1 cup dry white wine (optional)
- 2 medium potatoes, peeled and diced
- 1 bay leaf
- 1 teaspoon dried thyme
- 1 teaspoon dried basil
- 1/2 teaspoon paprika
- Salt and freshly ground black pepper, to taste
- 2 cans (6.5 ounces each) chopped clams, drained (reserve the juice)
- 1 cup frozen or fresh corn kernels (optional)
- 1/2 cup fresh parsley, chopped (for garnish)

**Instructions:**

1. **Cook the Bacon:**
   - In a large pot or Dutch oven, cook the chopped bacon over medium heat until crispy. Remove the bacon with a slotted spoon and set aside, leaving the bacon fat in the pot.
2. **Sauté Vegetables:**
   - Add the chopped onion, garlic, celery, bell pepper, and carrots to the pot. Sauté until the vegetables are tender, about 5-7 minutes.
3. **Add Tomatoes and Liquid:**
   - Stir in the diced tomatoes (with their juice) and tomato paste. Cook for another 2 minutes.
   - Pour in the clam juice (or seafood stock) and white wine, if using. Stir to combine.
4. **Add Potatoes and Seasonings:**
   - Add the diced potatoes, bay leaf, thyme, basil, paprika, salt, and pepper. Bring to a boil, then reduce the heat to a simmer.
   - Cover and cook for about 15-20 minutes, or until the potatoes are tender.
5. **Add Clams and Corn:**
   - Stir in the chopped clams and frozen corn (if using). Simmer for an additional 5 minutes, until the clams are heated through and the corn is cooked.
6. **Finish and Serve:**

- Adjust seasoning with additional salt and pepper if needed.
- Remove the bay leaf and discard.
- Ladle the chowder into bowls and garnish with the crispy bacon and chopped parsley.

Serve your Manhattan Clam Chowder hot, with crusty bread or oyster crackers on the side. Enjoy this hearty, flavorful chowder!

**New York-style Hot Dogs**

**Ingredients:**

- **For the Hot Dogs:**
    - 4 beef hot dogs (preferably all-beef franks)
    - 4 hot dog buns
    - 1 cup sauerkraut (optional, for topping)
    - Yellow mustard (for topping)
    - Pickle relish (optional, for topping)
- **For the Onions (optional but traditional):**
    - 1 large onion, finely chopped
    - 1 tablespoon vegetable oil
    - 1/2 cup beef or chicken broth
    - 1 tablespoon tomato paste
    - 1 teaspoon paprika
    - Salt and pepper to taste

**Instructions:**

1. **Prepare the Onions (Optional):**
    - Heat the vegetable oil in a small skillet over medium heat.
    - Add the chopped onion and cook, stirring occasionally, until softened and golden brown, about 5-7 minutes.
    - Stir in the tomato paste and paprika. Cook for another 2 minutes.
    - Add the broth, bring to a simmer, and cook until the mixture thickens slightly, about 10 minutes. Season with salt and pepper to taste.
    - Keep warm until ready to use.
2. **Cook the Hot Dogs:**
    - **Boil Method:**
        - Fill a medium pot with water and bring to a boil.
        - Add the hot dogs and reduce the heat to a simmer.
        - Cook for 5-7 minutes, or until the hot dogs are heated through.
    - **Grill Method:**
        - Preheat your grill to medium heat.
        - Grill the hot dogs for 5-7 minutes, turning occasionally, until heated through and slightly charred.
3. **Prepare the Buns:**
    - If desired, lightly toast the hot dog buns on the grill or in a toaster for added texture.
4. **Assemble the Hot Dogs:**
    - Place each hot dog in a bun.
    - Top with yellow mustard, sauerkraut, and the onion mixture (if using). You can also add pickle relish if desired.
5. **Serve:**

- - Serve the hot dogs immediately with additional condiments or toppings as desired.

Enjoy your homemade New York-style hot dogs with classic toppings and a touch of NYC street food nostalgia!

**Chicken and Rice from the Halal Cart**

**Ingredients:**

- **For the Chicken Marinade:**
    - 1 pound boneless, skinless chicken thighs (or breasts)
    - 1/4 cup plain Greek yogurt
    - 2 tablespoons olive oil
    - 2 tablespoons lemon juice
    - 3 cloves garlic, minced
    - 1 tablespoon ground cumin
    - 1 tablespoon ground coriander
    - 1 teaspoon paprika
    - 1/2 teaspoon ground turmeric
    - 1/2 teaspoon ground cinnamon
    - 1/2 teaspoon ground black pepper
    - 1 teaspoon salt
- **For the Rice:**
    - 1 cup basmati rice
    - 1 1/2 cups water
    - 1 tablespoon olive oil
    - 1/2 teaspoon ground cumin
    - 1/2 teaspoon ground turmeric
    - 1/4 teaspoon salt
- **For the White Sauce:**
    - 1/2 cup mayonnaise
    - 1/4 cup plain Greek yogurt
    - 1 tablespoon lemon juice
    - 1 teaspoon garlic powder
    - 1 teaspoon dried dill (optional)
    - Salt and black pepper to taste
- **For the Salad (Optional):**
    - 1 cup shredded lettuce
    - 1/2 cup cherry tomatoes, halved
    - 1/2 cucumber, sliced
    - 1/4 red onion, thinly sliced
    - 1 tablespoon olive oil
    - 1 tablespoon lemon juice
    - Salt and pepper to taste

**Instructions:**

1. **Marinate the Chicken:**
    - In a large bowl, combine the Greek yogurt, olive oil, lemon juice, garlic, cumin, coriander, paprika, turmeric, cinnamon, black pepper, and salt.

- Add the chicken thighs and coat them well with the marinade. Cover and refrigerate for at least 1 hour, or overnight for best results.

2. **Cook the Chicken:**
    - Preheat a grill or skillet over medium-high heat.
    - Grill or cook the chicken for about 6-8 minutes per side, or until fully cooked and the internal temperature reaches 165°F (74°C).
    - Let the chicken rest for a few minutes before slicing into strips or chunks.
3. **Prepare the Rice:**
    - Rinse the basmati rice under cold water until the water runs clear.
    - In a medium pot, heat the olive oil over medium heat.
    - Add the rinsed rice, cumin, turmeric, and salt. Stir for a minute to toast the rice lightly.
    - Add the water, bring to a boil, then reduce the heat to low. Cover and simmer for about 15-20 minutes, or until the rice is tender and the water is absorbed. Fluff with a fork.
4. **Prepare the White Sauce:**
    - In a small bowl, whisk together the mayonnaise, Greek yogurt, lemon juice, garlic powder, and dried dill (if using). Season with salt and pepper to taste.
5. **Prepare the Salad (Optional):**
    - In a bowl, combine the shredded lettuce, cherry tomatoes, cucumber, and red onion.
    - Drizzle with olive oil and lemon juice, and season with salt and pepper. Toss to combine.
6. **Assemble the Dish:**
    - Serve the cooked chicken over a bed of rice.
    - Drizzle with the white sauce and add a side of salad if desired.

This recipe captures the essence of the popular Halal Cart dish with flavorful chicken, fragrant rice, and creamy white sauce. Enjoy your homemade Chicken and Rice with a touch of NYC street food flavor!

**Corned Beef Hash**

**Ingredients:**

- 1 tablespoon vegetable oil
- 1 medium onion, finely chopped
- 2 cloves garlic, minced
- 2 cups cooked corned beef, diced (preferably leftover or from a can)
- 2 cups cooked potatoes, diced (you can use leftover or pre-cooked potatoes)
- 1/2 cup bell pepper, finely chopped (optional)
- 1 teaspoon paprika
- 1/2 teaspoon dried thyme
- 1/4 teaspoon black pepper
- 1/2 teaspoon salt (or to taste)
- 2 tablespoons fresh parsley, chopped (for garnish)
- 4 large eggs (optional, for serving)

**Instructions:**

1. **Prepare the Ingredients:**
    - If you're using leftover corned beef, dice it into small cubes. If using canned corned beef, break it up into chunks.
    - Dice the cooked potatoes and chop the onion, garlic, and bell pepper (if using).
2. **Cook the Onion and Garlic:**
    - Heat the vegetable oil in a large skillet over medium heat.
    - Add the chopped onion and cook, stirring occasionally, until softened and translucent, about 5-7 minutes.
    - Add the minced garlic and cook for another 1 minute.
3. **Add Corned Beef and Potatoes:**
    - Stir in the diced corned beef and cook for 5 minutes, allowing it to brown slightly.
    - Add the diced potatoes and bell pepper (if using), and cook for another 10-15 minutes, stirring occasionally. You want the potatoes to become crispy and browned in some spots.
4. **Season:**
    - Season the hash with paprika, dried thyme, black pepper, and salt. Stir well to combine and allow the flavors to meld together.
5. **Optional: Add Eggs:**
    - If desired, you can top the hash with eggs. To do this, make small wells in the hash mixture and crack an egg into each well.
    - Cover the skillet with a lid and cook over low heat until the eggs are cooked to your liking (about 5-7 minutes for sunny-side up eggs).
6. **Serve:**
    - Garnish the hash with chopped fresh parsley.
    - Serve hot, with or without eggs, and enjoy!

Corned Beef Hash is a versatile dish that can be enjoyed on its own or with a variety of sides like toast, biscuits, or a simple green salad.

**New York-style Knish**

**Ingredients:**

- **For the Dough:**
    - 3 cups all-purpose flour
    - 1/2 teaspoon salt
    - 1 cup unsalted butter, chilled and cut into small pieces
    - 1 large egg
    - 1/2 cup cold water (more if needed)
- **For the Potato Filling:**
    - 2 large russet potatoes, peeled and diced
    - 1 large onion, finely chopped
    - 2 tablespoons unsalted butter
    - 1/2 cup milk
    - 1/2 teaspoon salt
    - 1/4 teaspoon black pepper
    - 1/4 teaspoon ground paprika (optional)
    - 1 large egg, beaten (for egg wash)

**Instructions:**

1. **Prepare the Dough:**
    - In a large bowl, combine the flour and salt.
    - Add the chilled butter pieces and use a pastry cutter or your fingers to cut the butter into the flour until the mixture resembles coarse crumbs.
    - In a small bowl, whisk together the egg and cold water.
    - Add the egg mixture to the flour mixture and stir until a dough forms. If the dough is too dry, add a little more cold water, one tablespoon at a time.
    - Divide the dough into two equal parts, shape each into a disk, wrap in plastic wrap, and refrigerate for at least 30 minutes.
2. **Prepare the Potato Filling:**
    - In a large pot, bring water to a boil and add the diced potatoes. Cook until tender, about 15 minutes. Drain well.
    - In a skillet, melt the butter over medium heat. Add the chopped onion and cook until softened and golden brown, about 5-7 minutes.
    - Mash the cooked potatoes and mix in the sautéed onions, milk, salt, pepper, and paprika (if using). The mixture should be smooth and spreadable. Let it cool slightly.
3. **Assemble the Knishes:**
    - Preheat your oven to 375°F (190°C). Line a baking sheet with parchment paper.
    - On a lightly floured surface, roll out one disk of dough to about 1/8-inch thickness.
    - Cut the dough into rectangles, approximately 4x6 inches.

- Place a spoonful of potato filling in the center of each rectangle, leaving a border around the edges.
- Fold the dough over the filling to form a pocket and press the edges to seal. You can use a fork to crimp the edges for a decorative touch.
- Repeat with the remaining dough and filling.
- Brush the tops of the knishes with the beaten egg for a shiny finish.

4. **Bake:**
   - Place the knishes on the prepared baking sheet and bake in the preheated oven for 25-30 minutes, or until golden brown and crispy.

5. **Serve:**
   - Allow the knishes to cool slightly before serving. They can be enjoyed warm or at room temperature.

New York-style Knishes are perfect for a snack, lunch, or as part of a larger meal. Enjoy the flaky pastry and savory potato filling!

**Spicy Sausage and Pepper Hero**

**Ingredients:**

- **For the Sausages:**
    - 4 Italian spicy sausages (pork or turkey)
    - 1 tablespoon olive oil
- **For the Peppers and Onions:**
    - 2 tablespoons olive oil
    - 1 large onion, thinly sliced
    - 1 red bell pepper, thinly sliced
    - 1 yellow bell pepper, thinly sliced
    - 1 green bell pepper, thinly sliced
    - 2 cloves garlic, minced
    - 1/2 teaspoon dried oregano
    - 1/2 teaspoon dried basil
    - Salt and freshly ground black pepper, to taste
    - 1/4 teaspoon red pepper flakes (optional, for extra heat)
- **For the Assembly:**
    - 4 hoagie rolls or sub rolls
    - 1/2 cup marinara sauce or tomato sauce (optional)
    - Grated Parmesan cheese (optional)

**Instructions:**

1. **Cook the Sausages:**
    - Preheat your grill or a skillet over medium-high heat.
    - Lightly brush the sausages with olive oil.
    - Grill or cook the sausages, turning occasionally, until they are fully cooked and have a nice char, about 10-12 minutes. The internal temperature should reach 160°F (71°C).
    - Once cooked, remove from heat and let rest for a few minutes before slicing them into bite-sized pieces if desired.
2. **Prepare the Peppers and Onions:**
    - In a large skillet, heat the olive oil over medium heat.
    - Add the sliced onions and cook until softened and slightly caramelized, about 8-10 minutes.
    - Add the bell peppers and cook for another 5 minutes until they are tender but still slightly crisp.
    - Stir in the minced garlic, oregano, basil, salt, pepper, and red pepper flakes (if using). Cook for another 2 minutes, until the garlic is fragrant and the flavors are well combined.
    - Adjust seasoning to taste.
3. **Assemble the Hero Sandwiches:**
    - If you're using marinara sauce, lightly toast the hoagie rolls in a toaster or oven.

- If desired, spread a thin layer of marinara sauce on the inside of each roll.
- Place a portion of the sausage pieces on the bottom half of each roll.
- Top with the sautéed peppers and onions.
- Sprinkle with grated Parmesan cheese if desired.

4. **Serve:**
    - Serve the Spicy Sausage and Pepper Heroes hot and enjoy!

These sandwiches are hearty, flavorful, and perfect for a satisfying meal. Whether you're enjoying them as a quick dinner or serving them at a casual gathering, they're sure to be a hit!

# Classic Reuben Sandwich

## Ingredients:

- 8 slices rye bread (preferably Jewish rye)
- 8 ounces sliced corned beef (about 1/2 pound)
- 4 ounces Swiss cheese, sliced (about 1/4 pound)
- 1 cup sauerkraut, drained and squeezed dry
- 4 tablespoons Russian dressing or Thousand Island dressing
- 2 tablespoons unsalted butter

## Instructions:

1. **Prepare the Ingredients:**
   - Drain and squeeze out excess moisture from the sauerkraut to prevent sogginess.
   - If using Russian or Thousand Island dressing, have it ready for spreading.
2. **Assemble the Sandwiches:**
   - Lay out 4 slices of rye bread on a clean surface.
   - Spread 1 tablespoon of dressing on each slice of bread.
   - On each slice of bread, layer the sliced Swiss cheese, followed by a generous portion of corned beef.
   - Top with a good amount of sauerkraut.
   - Place the remaining slices of rye bread on top to complete the sandwiches.
3. **Butter the Bread:**
   - Spread butter on the outside of each slice of bread. This will help the bread brown and become crispy when grilling.
4. **Grill the Sandwiches:**
   - Heat a skillet or griddle over medium heat.
   - Place the sandwiches in the skillet, buttered side down. Cook until the bread is golden brown and crispy, about 3-4 minutes.
   - Flip the sandwiches and cook the other side until golden brown and the cheese is melted, another 3-4 minutes.
   - If needed, you can cover the skillet with a lid for a minute to help melt the cheese faster.
5. **Serve:**
   - Remove the sandwiches from the skillet and let them rest for a minute before cutting in half.
   - Serve hot with a side of pickle spears and additional dressing for dipping if desired.

Enjoy your Classic Reuben Sandwich with its perfectly melted cheese, tangy sauerkraut, and deliciously crispy bread!

NYC Pretzels

**Ingredients:**

- **For the Pretzel Dough:**
    - 1 1/2 cups warm water (110°F or 45°C)
    - 1 packet active dry yeast (2 1/4 teaspoons)
    - 1 tablespoon granulated sugar
    - 4 cups all-purpose flour
    - 1 teaspoon salt
    - 1/4 cup unsalted butter, melted
- **For the Boiling Solution:**
    - 10 cups water
    - 2/3 cup baking soda
- **For the Topping:**
    - 1 large egg, beaten (for egg wash)
    - Coarse sea salt or pretzel salt (for sprinkling)

**Instructions:**

1. **Prepare the Dough:**
    - In a small bowl, dissolve the sugar in the warm water. Sprinkle the yeast over the top and let it sit for about 5 minutes, or until foamy.
    - In a large mixing bowl, combine the flour and salt. Make a well in the center and pour in the yeast mixture and melted butter.
    - Stir until the dough begins to come together, then knead on a lightly floured surface for about 5-7 minutes, or until the dough is smooth and elastic.
    - Place the dough in a lightly oiled bowl, cover with a damp cloth or plastic wrap, and let it rise in a warm place for about 1 hour, or until doubled in size.
2. **Preheat the Oven and Prepare the Boiling Solution:**
    - Preheat your oven to 450°F (230°C). Line two baking sheets with parchment paper or lightly grease them.
    - In a large pot, bring the 10 cups of water to a boil. Once boiling, carefully add the baking soda. The solution will bubble up, so stir gently.
3. **Shape the Pretzels:**
    - Punch down the risen dough and divide it into 8 equal pieces.
    - Roll each piece into a long rope, about 18 inches in length. Form each rope into a U-shape, then twist the ends together and press them onto the bottom of the U to form a pretzel shape.
    - Carefully lower each pretzel into the boiling baking soda solution for about 30 seconds, then remove with a slotted spoon and place on the prepared baking sheets.
4. **Apply the Egg Wash and Bake:**
    - Brush each pretzel with the beaten egg and sprinkle with coarse sea salt.
    - Bake in the preheated oven for 12-15 minutes, or until the pretzels are deep brown and crispy.
5. **Cool and Serve:**

- Allow the pretzels to cool slightly on a wire rack before serving.
- Enjoy your NYC pretzels warm with mustard or your favorite dipping sauce.

These pretzels are perfect for a snack or as part of a casual meal. The baking soda bath gives them that distinctive flavor and color reminiscent of New York City street pretzels.

**Lobster Roll**

**Ingredients:**

- 2 cups cooked lobster meat, chopped (from about 2 lobster tails or equivalent)
- 1/4 cup mayonnaise
- 1 tablespoon fresh lemon juice
- 1 tablespoon fresh chives or celery, finely chopped
- Salt and freshly ground black pepper, to taste
- 4 top-split hot dog buns or rolls
- 2 tablespoons unsalted butter

**Instructions:**

1. **Prepare the Lobster Salad:**
   - In a large bowl, combine the chopped lobster meat, mayonnaise, lemon juice, and chives or celery.
   - Season with salt and pepper to taste. Mix gently to combine, being careful not to break up the lobster meat too much.
2. **Prepare the Buns:**
   - Heat a skillet over medium heat. Spread butter on the outside of each hot dog bun.
   - Toast the buns in the skillet until golden brown and crispy on the outside, about 2-3 minutes per side.
3. **Assemble the Lobster Rolls:**
   - Fill each toasted bun with a generous amount of the lobster salad.
4. **Serve:**
   - Serve immediately, garnished with extra chives or a lemon wedge if desired.

## Connecticut-Style Lobster Roll

**Ingredients:**

- 2 cups cooked lobster meat, chopped (from about 2 lobster tails or equivalent)
- 4 tablespoons unsalted butter
- 1 tablespoon fresh lemon juice
- Salt and freshly ground black pepper, to taste
- 4 top-split hot dog buns or rolls

**Instructions:**

1. **Prepare the Lobster Filling:**
   - In a large skillet, melt the butter over medium heat.
   - Add the chopped lobster meat and lemon juice. Toss gently to coat the lobster in the melted butter.

- Cook for 2-3 minutes until the lobster is heated through. Season with salt and pepper to taste.
2. **Prepare the Buns:**
    - Heat a separate skillet over medium heat. Spread butter on the outside of each hot dog bun.
    - Toast the buns in the skillet until golden brown and crispy on the outside, about 2-3 minutes per side.
3. **Assemble the Lobster Rolls:**
    - Spoon the warm lobster and butter mixture into each toasted bun.
4. **Serve:**
    - Serve immediately with a side of coleslaw or potato chips if desired.

Both styles of Lobster Roll highlight the lobster's sweet flavor and tender texture. Enjoy these rolls as a special treat or for a taste of New England cuisine!

# New York-style Bialys

**Ingredients:**

- **For the Dough:**
    - 1 cup warm water (110°F or 45°C)
    - 1 packet active dry yeast (2 1/4 teaspoons)
    - 1 tablespoon granulated sugar
    - 3 1/2 cups all-purpose flour
    - 1 1/2 teaspoons salt
    - 2 tablespoons vegetable oil
- **For the Filling:**
    - 1 tablespoon vegetable oil
    - 1 large onion, finely chopped
    - 2 cloves garlic, minced (optional)
    - 2 tablespoons poppy seeds
    - 1/2 teaspoon salt
    - 1/4 teaspoon black pepper
- **For the Topping:**
    - 1 egg, beaten (for egg wash)
    - Additional poppy seeds for sprinkling

**Instructions:**

1. **Prepare the Dough:**
    - In a small bowl, dissolve the sugar in the warm water. Sprinkle the yeast over the top and let it sit for about 5 minutes, or until foamy.
    - In a large mixing bowl, combine the flour and salt. Make a well in the center and pour in the yeast mixture and vegetable oil.
    - Mix until a dough forms, then turn out onto a floured surface and knead for about 8-10 minutes, until the dough is smooth and elastic.
    - Place the dough in a lightly oiled bowl, cover with a damp cloth or plastic wrap, and let it rise in a warm place for about 1 hour, or until doubled in size.
2. **Prepare the Filling:**
    - In a skillet, heat the vegetable oil over medium heat.
    - Add the chopped onion and cook, stirring occasionally, until softened and lightly caramelized, about 10 minutes. Add garlic if using, and cook for another minute.
    - Remove from heat and stir in the poppy seeds, salt, and pepper. Let the filling cool to room temperature.
3. **Shape the Bialys:**
    - Preheat your oven to 425°F (220°C) and line a baking sheet with parchment paper.
    - Punch down the risen dough and divide it into 8-10 equal pieces. Shape each piece into a ball and place them on the prepared baking sheet.

- Using your fingers, gently press down in the center of each ball to create a well. You can use the back of a spoon to help shape the well, but avoid pressing all the way through.
- Spoon a small amount of the onion filling into each well, smoothing it out slightly.

4. **Prepare for Baking:**
   - Brush the tops of the bialys with the beaten egg and sprinkle with additional poppy seeds.
5. **Bake:**
   - Bake in the preheated oven for 15-20 minutes, or until the bialys are golden brown and the edges are crisp.
6. **Cool and Serve:**
   - Let the bialys cool on a wire rack before serving.

New York-style Bialys are perfect for breakfast, brunch, or as a delicious snack. Enjoy them fresh and warm from the oven or toasted with a bit of butter.

# Cheesesteak

## Ingredients:

- **For the Steak:**
    - 1 pound ribeye or sirloin steak, thinly sliced (freeze the steak for about 30 minutes for easier slicing)
    - 1 tablespoon vegetable oil
    - Salt and freshly ground black pepper, to taste
- **For the Toppings:**
    - 1 large onion, thinly sliced
    - 1 large green bell pepper, thinly sliced (optional)
    - 2 cloves garlic, minced (optional)
    - 4 slices provolone cheese, American cheese, or Cheez Whiz (traditional choices)
    - 4 hoagie rolls or Italian sub rolls

## Instructions:

1. **Prepare the Steak:**
    - Thinly slice the steak against the grain. If needed, you can slightly freeze the steak to make slicing easier.
    - Season the sliced steak with salt and pepper.
2. **Cook the Vegetables:**
    - Heat 1 tablespoon of vegetable oil in a large skillet over medium heat.
    - Add the onions and bell peppers (if using) and cook, stirring occasionally, until softened and slightly caramelized, about 8-10 minutes.
    - Add the minced garlic (if using) and cook for an additional minute. Remove the vegetables from the skillet and set aside.
3. **Cook the Steak:**
    - In the same skillet, add a little more oil if needed and increase the heat to medium-high.
    - Add the sliced steak in a single layer. Cook for about 2-3 minutes without stirring to get a good sear, then stir and cook until the steak is cooked through, about another 2-3 minutes. Adjust seasoning with more salt and pepper if necessary.
4. **Combine Steak and Vegetables:**
    - Return the cooked onions and peppers to the skillet with the steak and stir to combine. Cook for an additional minute or two until everything is heated through.
5. **Assemble the Sandwiches:**
    - Preheat your oven to 350°F (175°C). Slice the hoagie rolls open, but do not cut all the way through, leaving them hinged.
    - Divide the steak and vegetable mixture evenly among the rolls.
    - Place the cheese slices on top of the steak mixture. If using Cheez Whiz, you can warm it in the microwave or on the stove and spoon it over the steak.
    - Place the filled rolls on a baking sheet and bake in the preheated oven for about 5 minutes, or until the cheese is melted and the rolls are slightly toasted.

6. **Serve:**
    - Remove from the oven and serve hot.

**Optional Additions:**

- **Mushrooms:** Sautéed mushrooms can be added to the filling for extra flavor.
- **Hot Peppers:** For a spicy kick, add sliced hot peppers or jalapeños.

Enjoy your homemade Cheesesteak with a side of fries or a simple salad!

**Creamy New York-style Rice Pudding**

**Ingredients:**

- 1 cup Arborio rice or short-grain rice
- 2 cups whole milk
- 1 cup heavy cream
- 1/2 cup granulated sugar
- 1/4 teaspoon salt
- 1/2 teaspoon vanilla extract
- 1/4 teaspoon ground cinnamon (optional)
- 1/4 cup raisins or sultanas (optional)
- Ground nutmeg for garnish (optional)

**Instructions:**

1. **Prepare the Rice:**
    - Rinse the rice under cold water until the water runs clear. This helps remove excess starch and prevents the pudding from becoming too thick.
2. **Cook the Rice:**
    - In a medium saucepan, combine the rinsed rice and 2 cups of water. Bring to a boil over medium-high heat.
    - Reduce the heat to low, cover, and simmer for about 15-20 minutes, or until the rice is tender and most of the water has been absorbed.
3. **Make the Pudding:**
    - Add the milk, heavy cream, sugar, and salt to the saucepan with the cooked rice.
    - Cook over medium heat, stirring frequently, until the mixture begins to thicken and the rice is fully cooked, about 15-20 minutes.
    - If using raisins or sultanas, add them to the saucepan in the last 5 minutes of cooking.
4. **Finish the Pudding:**
    - Once the pudding has reached your desired consistency, remove the saucepan from the heat.
    - Stir in the vanilla extract and ground cinnamon if using.
5. **Serve:**
    - Transfer the pudding to serving bowls or individual cups. If desired, garnish with a sprinkle of ground nutmeg.
    - The rice pudding can be served warm, at room temperature, or chilled. It will thicken further as it cools.

**Tips:**

- **Consistency:** If the pudding is too thick after cooling, you can stir in a little more milk or cream to reach your desired consistency.

- **Flavor Variations:** For additional flavor, you can add a pinch of cardamom, a splash of almond extract, or fresh fruit such as berries.

Enjoy your creamy New York-style rice pudding, a classic dessert that's perfect for any occasion!

# New York-style Roast Beef Sandwich

## Ingredients:

- **For the Sandwich:**
    - 1 pound thinly sliced roast beef (preferably from a deli or homemade)
    - 4 crusty rolls or hoagie rolls (e.g., Italian rolls, ciabatta, or kaiser rolls)
    - 4 tablespoons horseradish sauce or prepared horseradish (optional)
    - 4 tablespoons mayonnaise (optional)
    - 4 tablespoons Dijon mustard or yellow mustard (optional)
    - 1 cup thinly sliced pickles
    - 1 large onion, thinly sliced
    - 1 cup shredded lettuce
    - 4 slices Swiss cheese or American cheese (optional)
    - Salt and freshly ground black pepper, to taste

## Instructions:

1. **Prepare the Ingredients:**
    - If you have a roast beef that needs to be warmed, you can heat it up gently in a skillet over medium heat or in the oven at a low temperature. If using deli-sliced roast beef, it's usually ready to go.
    - Slice the rolls open, but do not cut all the way through, leaving them hinged.
2. **Toast the Rolls (optional):**
    - For a crispy texture, lightly toast the inside of the rolls under a broiler or in a toaster oven.
3. **Assemble the Sandwiches:**
    - Spread horseradish sauce or prepared horseradish on one side of the roll if using.
    - Spread mayonnaise and/or Dijon mustard on the other side of the roll if desired.
    - Layer the sliced roast beef generously onto the bottom half of each roll.
    - Add a slice of Swiss or American cheese on top of the beef if using.
    - Top with thinly sliced onions, pickles, and shredded lettuce.
    - Season with a bit of salt and freshly ground black pepper to taste.
4. **Serve:**
    - Close the sandwiches and cut in half if desired.
    - Serve immediately with your choice of sides such as potato chips, coleslaw, or a pickle spear.

## Tips:

- **Roast Beef:** For an authentic taste, use well-seasoned roast beef, either from a deli or made at home. If making at home, season a beef roast with salt, pepper, and garlic, then roast it in the oven until medium-rare to medium, and slice thinly.

- **Variations:** Add sautéed mushrooms, bell peppers, or a slice of tomato for extra flavor and texture.
- **Horseradish:** Adjust the amount of horseradish according to your taste preference. For a milder version, use less, or omit it if preferred.

Enjoy your classic New York-style roast beef sandwich, a satisfying and flavorful choice for lunch or a hearty meal!

# Garlic Knots

## Ingredients:

- **For the Dough:**
  - 1 pound pizza dough (store-bought or homemade)
- **For the Garlic Butter:**
  - 1/2 cup unsalted butter (1 stick)
  - 4 cloves garlic, minced
  - 2 tablespoons fresh parsley, finely chopped (or 1 tablespoon dried parsley)
  - 1/4 teaspoon salt
  - 1/4 teaspoon crushed red pepper flakes (optional, for a bit of heat)
- **For Garnish:**
  - Additional chopped parsley for sprinkling
  - Grated Parmesan cheese (optional)

## Instructions:

1. **Prepare the Dough:**
   - Preheat your oven to 400°F (200°C). Line a baking sheet with parchment paper or lightly grease it.
   - If using store-bought pizza dough, let it come to room temperature if it's been refrigerated. If making your own dough, follow your preferred recipe.
2. **Shape the Knots:**
   - On a lightly floured surface, roll out the pizza dough into a rectangle about 1/2 inch thick.
   - Cut the dough into strips, approximately 1 inch wide and 6 inches long.
   - Take each strip and tie it into a knot, tucking the ends underneath to secure them. Place the knots on the prepared baking sheet.
3. **Bake the Knots:**
   - Bake in the preheated oven for 12-15 minutes, or until the knots are golden brown and cooked through.
4. **Prepare the Garlic Butter:**
   - While the knots are baking, melt the butter in a small saucepan over medium heat.
   - Add the minced garlic and cook for 1-2 minutes, just until fragrant (do not let it brown).
   - Stir in the chopped parsley, salt, and crushed red pepper flakes if using. Remove from heat.
5. **Finish the Knots:**
   - As soon as the knots come out of the oven, brush them generously with the garlic butter mixture.
   - If desired, sprinkle with additional chopped parsley and grated Parmesan cheese.
6. **Serve:**
   - Serve the garlic knots warm, straight from the oven, as an appetizer or side dish.

**Tips:**

- **Dough:** If you have leftover pizza dough, you can freeze it for future use or repurpose it into other bread recipes.
- **Garlic Butter:** For a stronger garlic flavor, you can increase the number of garlic cloves or let it simmer for a bit longer, but be careful not to burn it.

Enjoy your homemade Garlic Knots with marinara sauce for dipping or simply on their own!

**Brooklyn-style Pizza**

**Ingredients:**

- **For the Dough:**
    - 3 1/2 cups all-purpose flour
    - 1 1/2 teaspoons salt
    - 1 teaspoon sugar
    - 1 packet active dry yeast (2 1/4 teaspoons)
    - 1 1/4 cups warm water (110°F or 45°C)
    - 2 tablespoons olive oil
- **For the Sauce:**
    - 1 can (15 ounces) crushed tomatoes
    - 1/4 cup tomato paste
    - 1 tablespoon olive oil
    - 2 cloves garlic, minced
    - 1 teaspoon dried oregano
    - 1/2 teaspoon dried basil
    - 1/4 teaspoon red pepper flakes (optional)
    - Salt and freshly ground black pepper, to taste
- **For the Toppings:**
    - 2 cups shredded mozzarella cheese
    - 1/2 cup grated Parmesan cheese
    - Your choice of toppings (e.g., pepperoni, sausage, mushrooms, bell peppers, onions, olives, etc.)

**Instructions:**

1. **Prepare the Dough:**
    - In a small bowl, dissolve the sugar in the warm water. Sprinkle the yeast over the top and let it sit for about 5 minutes, or until foamy.
    - In a large mixing bowl, combine the flour and salt. Make a well in the center and pour in the yeast mixture and olive oil.
    - Mix until the dough begins to come together, then turn out onto a floured surface and knead for about 8-10 minutes, or until the dough is smooth and elastic.
    - Place the dough in a lightly oiled bowl, cover with plastic wrap or a damp cloth, and let it rise in a warm place for about 1-2 hours, or until doubled in size.
2. **Prepare the Sauce:**
    - In a medium saucepan, heat the olive oil over medium heat. Add the minced garlic and cook until fragrant, about 1 minute.
    - Add the crushed tomatoes, tomato paste, oregano, basil, red pepper flakes (if using), salt, and pepper.
    - Simmer for 15-20 minutes, stirring occasionally, until the sauce has thickened. Adjust seasoning to taste.
3. **Preheat the Oven:**
    - Preheat your oven to 500°F (260°C). If using a pizza stone, place it in the oven to preheat as well. If not using a pizza stone, a baking sheet will work.

4. **Shape the Dough:**
   - Punch down the risen dough and divide it into 2 equal pieces for larger pizzas or 4 pieces for smaller pizzas.
   - On a floured surface, roll out each piece of dough into a thin round, about 12 inches in diameter, or as thin as you prefer. Transfer the rolled dough to a parchment-lined baking sheet or preheated pizza stone.
5. **Assemble the Pizza:**
   - Spread a thin layer of sauce over the dough, leaving a small border around the edges.
   - Sprinkle shredded mozzarella cheese evenly over the sauce.
   - Add your desired toppings, then sprinkle with grated Parmesan cheese.
6. **Bake the Pizza:**
   - Bake in the preheated oven for 10-15 minutes, or until the crust is golden brown and crispy and the cheese is melted and bubbly.
7. **Serve:**
   - Allow the pizza to cool slightly before slicing. Serve hot and enjoy!

**Tips:**

- **Dough Texture:** Brooklyn-style pizza dough is typically thin and crispy. If you prefer a softer crust, you can roll the dough a bit thicker.
- **Toppings:** Be generous with toppings but avoid overloading the pizza to ensure the crust remains crispy.
- **Stone vs. Sheet:** Baking on a pizza stone will give you a more evenly cooked and crispy crust, but a baking sheet works well too.

Enjoy your homemade Brooklyn-style pizza, a slice of New York's beloved pizza tradition right in your own kitchen!

**Lemon Ricotta Pancakes**

**Ingredients:**

- **For the Pancake Batter:**
    - 1 cup all-purpose flour
    - 2 tablespoons granulated sugar
    - 1 tablespoon baking powder
    - 1/2 teaspoon salt
    - 1 cup ricotta cheese
    - 1 cup milk
    - 2 large eggs
    - 1 tablespoon lemon zest (from about 1 lemon)
    - 1 tablespoon fresh lemon juice
    - 1/2 teaspoon vanilla extract
- **For Cooking:**
    - 2 tablespoons unsalted butter or oil (for greasing the griddle/pan)
- **For Serving:**
    - Maple syrup, fresh berries, or a dusting of powdered sugar (optional)

**Instructions:**

1. **Prepare the Dry Ingredients:**
    - In a large bowl, whisk together the flour, sugar, baking powder, and salt.
2. **Prepare the Wet Ingredients:**
    - In another bowl, combine the ricotta cheese, milk, eggs, lemon zest, lemon juice, and vanilla extract. Mix until well combined.
3. **Combine the Ingredients:**
    - Add the wet ingredients to the dry ingredients and gently stir until just combined. The batter will be thick, but avoid over-mixing; it's okay if there are a few lumps.
4. **Preheat the Pan or Griddle:**
    - Heat a griddle or non-stick skillet over medium heat and lightly grease with butter or oil.
5. **Cook the Pancakes:**
    - For each pancake, pour about 1/4 cup of batter onto the griddle. Cook until bubbles form on the surface and the edges look set, about 2-3 minutes. Flip the pancake and cook until the other side is golden brown, about 1-2 minutes more.
    - Repeat with the remaining batter, adding more butter or oil to the pan as needed.
6. **Serve:**
    - Serve the pancakes warm with your choice of toppings such as maple syrup, fresh berries, or a dusting of powdered sugar.

**Tips:**

- **Ricotta Cheese:** For best results, use whole-milk ricotta cheese. It provides a creamier texture compared to part-skim ricotta.

- **Lemon Zest:** Fresh lemon zest adds a bright, aromatic flavor. Be sure to zest only the yellow part of the lemon peel, as the white pith can be bitter.
- **Batter Consistency:** If the batter is too thick, you can thin it with a bit more milk.

These Lemon Ricotta Pancakes are perfect for a special breakfast or brunch, offering a light and fluffy texture with a burst of citrus flavor. Enjoy!

**Eggplant Parmesan Hero**

**Ingredients:**

- **For the Eggplant:**
    - 1 large eggplant
    - 1 cup all-purpose flour
    - 2 large eggs
    - 1 cup breadcrumbs (preferably Italian-seasoned)
    - 1/2 cup grated Parmesan cheese
    - Salt and freshly ground black pepper
    - Vegetable oil (for frying)
- **For the Sandwich Assembly:**
    - 1 cup marinara sauce (store-bought or homemade)
    - 1 cup shredded mozzarella cheese
    - 1/2 cup grated Parmesan cheese
    - 4 hero rolls or Italian sub rolls
    - Fresh basil leaves (optional, for garnish)

**Instructions:**

1. **Prepare the Eggplant:**
    - Slice the eggplant into 1/4-inch thick rounds. Sprinkle with salt and let them sit for about 30 minutes to draw out excess moisture. Rinse and pat dry with paper towels.
2. **Bread the Eggplant:**
    - Set up a breading station:
        - Place the flour in a shallow dish.
        - In a second dish, beat the eggs.
        - In a third dish, combine the breadcrumbs with 1/2 cup of grated Parmesan cheese.
    - Dredge each eggplant slice in the flour, shaking off excess.
    - Dip in the beaten eggs, allowing excess to drip off.
    - Coat with the breadcrumb mixture, pressing gently to adhere.
3. **Fry the Eggplant:**
    - Heat about 1/4 inch of vegetable oil in a large skillet over medium heat.
    - Fry the eggplant slices in batches, without overcrowding the pan, until golden brown and crispy, about 2-3 minutes per side.
    - Transfer to a paper towel-lined plate to drain excess oil. Season with salt while still hot.
4. **Preheat the Oven:**
    - Preheat your oven to 375°F (190°C).
5. **Assemble the Sandwiches:**
    - Slice the hero rolls lengthwise but not all the way through, leaving them hinged.
    - Spread a few tablespoons of marinara sauce on the bottom half of each roll.
    - Layer the fried eggplant slices over the sauce.
    - Spoon additional marinara sauce over the eggplant.

- Sprinkle shredded mozzarella cheese and additional grated Parmesan cheese on top.
6. **Bake:**
    - Place the assembled sandwiches on a baking sheet.
    - Bake in the preheated oven for about 10-15 minutes, or until the cheese is melted and bubbly and the rolls are toasted.
7. **Serve:**
    - Garnish with fresh basil leaves if desired.
    - Serve hot and enjoy!

**Tips:**

- **Breaded Eggplant:** For a lighter version, you can bake the breaded eggplant slices instead of frying. Place them on a baking sheet, brush with a bit of oil, and bake at 400°F (200°C) for 20-25 minutes, flipping halfway through.
- **Marinara Sauce:** Use your favorite marinara sauce, or make your own for a more personalized touch.
- **Cheese:** Feel free to experiment with other cheeses like provolone or fontina for different flavors.

Enjoy your Eggplant Parmesan Hero, a flavorful and satisfying sandwich perfect for lunch or dinner!

**NYC Deli Pickles**

**Ingredients:**

- **For the Pickles:**
    - 4-6 small to medium cucumbers (Kirby or Persian cucumbers work well)
    - 4 cloves garlic, peeled and smashed
    - 1 tablespoon whole black peppercorns
    - 1 tablespoon dill seeds or 2-3 sprigs fresh dill
    - 1 tablespoon mustard seeds (optional)
    - 1-2 bay leaves
    - 2 tablespoons kosher salt
    - 1 tablespoon sugar
    - 1 1/2 cups water
    - 1 cup white vinegar (or apple cider vinegar for a different flavor)

**Instructions:**

1. **Prepare the Cucumbers:**
    - Wash the cucumbers thoroughly. If they are larger, you may want to slice them into spears or halves to fit them into your jar more easily.
2. **Prepare the Brine:**
    - In a small saucepan, combine the water, vinegar, kosher salt, and sugar. Heat over medium heat, stirring occasionally, until the salt and sugar are fully dissolved. Remove from heat and let the brine cool to room temperature.
3. **Pack the Jars:**
    - Place the garlic cloves, peppercorns, dill seeds (or fresh dill), mustard seeds (if using), and bay leaves into clean, sterilized jars.
    - Pack the cucumbers tightly into the jars, making sure they fit snugly but are not crushed.
4. **Add the Brine:**
    - Pour the cooled brine over the cucumbers in the jars, making sure they are fully submerged. You might need to use a small plate or lid to weigh them down if they float above the brine.
5. **Seal and Refrigerate:**
    - Seal the jars with their lids and refrigerate. The pickles will begin to develop their flavor after about 24 hours but are best enjoyed after 2-3 days. They will continue to improve in flavor as they sit.
6. **Serve:**
    - Enjoy your homemade NYC deli pickles as a crunchy, tangy snack or as a perfect accompaniment to sandwiches and burgers.

**Tips:**

- **Cucumbers:** Use pickling cucumbers for the best results, as they have a firmer texture and better hold up to pickling.

- **Flavor Variations:** You can experiment with additional spices like red pepper flakes, coriander seeds, or celery seeds to customize the flavor.
- **Storage:** These pickles will keep in the refrigerator for up to 2-3 months.

Enjoy your homemade NYC deli pickles, a delightful and tangy treat that captures the essence of classic New York delis!

**Sweet and Sour Cabbage Soup**

**Ingredients:**

- 1 small head of cabbage, chopped
- 1 large onion, diced
- 2 cloves garlic, minced
- 2 carrots, peeled and sliced
- 1 large potato, peeled and diced
- 1 bell pepper, chopped
- 1 can (15 ounces) diced tomatoes
- 6 cups vegetable or chicken broth
- 1/4 cup apple cider vinegar
- 2 tablespoons granulated sugar
- 2 tablespoons olive oil
- 1 bay leaf
- 1 teaspoon dried thyme
- Salt and freshly ground black pepper, to taste
- Optional: 1/2 pound of smoked sausage or bacon, sliced (for added flavor)

**Instructions:**

1. **Prepare the Vegetables:**
    - Wash and chop the cabbage into bite-sized pieces. Dice the onion, mince the garlic, and slice the carrots and bell pepper. Peel and dice the potato.
2. **Cook the Meat (if using):**
    - In a large pot or Dutch oven, heat the olive oil over medium heat. If using smoked sausage or bacon, add it to the pot and cook until browned. Remove the meat and set aside, leaving the fat in the pot.
3. **Sauté the Vegetables:**
    - In the same pot, add the diced onion and cook until softened, about 3-4 minutes. Add the minced garlic and cook for an additional 1 minute.
    - Stir in the carrots, bell pepper, and potato, and cook for another 5 minutes.
4. **Add the Cabbage:**
    - Add the chopped cabbage to the pot and cook, stirring occasionally, until the cabbage starts to wilt, about 5 minutes.
5. **Add the Liquids and Seasonings:**
    - Pour in the diced tomatoes with their juices and the vegetable or chicken broth. Add the apple cider vinegar, sugar, bay leaf, and dried thyme. Stir to combine.
    - Return the cooked sausage or bacon to the pot, if using.
6. **Simmer the Soup:**
    - Bring the soup to a boil, then reduce the heat to low. Cover and let it simmer for 30-40 minutes, or until all the vegetables are tender and the flavors have melded together.
7. **Season and Serve:**
    - Taste the soup and adjust the seasoning with salt and freshly ground black pepper as needed.

- Serve hot, garnished with fresh parsley if desired.

**Tips:**

- **Flavor Balance:** Adjust the amount of sugar and vinegar to taste. Some people prefer a sweeter soup, while others might like it more tangy.
- **Add-ins:** Feel free to add other vegetables like celery or green beans, or even some cooked rice or pasta for a heartier soup.
- **Make Ahead:** This soup keeps well in the refrigerator for up to a week and often tastes even better the next day as the flavors continue to develop.

Enjoy your homemade Sweet and Sour Cabbage Soup, a comforting and flavorful dish perfect for any season!

**New York-style Buffalo Wings**

**Ingredients:**

- **For the Wings:**
    - 2 pounds chicken wings (drumettes and flats)
    - 1 teaspoon baking powder
    - 1/2 teaspoon salt
    - 1/2 teaspoon black pepper
    - 1/2 teaspoon garlic powder
    - 1/2 teaspoon onion powder
    - Vegetable oil (for frying)
- **For the Buffalo Sauce:**
    - 1/2 cup Frank's RedHot sauce (or your favorite hot sauce)
    - 1/4 cup unsalted butter
    - 1 tablespoon white vinegar
    - 1/4 teaspoon garlic powder
    - 1/4 teaspoon onion powder
    - 1/4 teaspoon paprika
    - 1/4 teaspoon cayenne pepper (optional, for extra heat)
    - Salt, to taste
- **For Serving:**
    - Celery sticks
    - Carrot sticks
    - Blue cheese or ranch dressing

**Instructions:**

1. **Prepare the Wings:**
    - Pat the chicken wings dry with paper towels. This helps achieve a crispy skin.
    - In a large bowl, toss the wings with the baking powder, salt, black pepper, garlic powder, and onion powder until evenly coated. The baking powder helps make the skin crispier.
2. **Bake the Wings (optional but recommended for extra crispiness):**
    - Preheat your oven to 250°F (120°C). Place a wire rack on a baking sheet and arrange the wings in a single layer on the rack.
    - Bake for 30 minutes to render out some fat and dry out the skin.
    - Increase the oven temperature to 425°F (220°C) and bake for an additional 30 minutes, or until the wings are crispy and golden brown. Turn them halfway through for even cooking.
3. If you prefer to fry the wings, skip the baking step and follow the frying instructions below.
4. **Fry the Wings (alternative to baking):**
    - Heat vegetable oil in a large pot or deep fryer to 375°F (190°C). You need enough oil to fully submerge the wings.
    - Fry the wings in batches, being careful not to overcrowd the pot. Cook for 8-10 minutes per batch, or until the wings are golden brown and crispy.

       - Remove the wings with a slotted spoon and drain on a paper towel-lined plate.
5. **Prepare the Buffalo Sauce:**
       - In a small saucepan, melt the butter over medium heat.
       - Stir in the hot sauce, white vinegar, garlic powder, onion powder, paprika, and cayenne pepper (if using).
       - Bring the sauce to a simmer, then remove from heat. Adjust seasoning with salt to taste.
6. **Coat the Wings:**
       - If you baked the wings, toss them in the Buffalo sauce in a large bowl until evenly coated.
       - If you fried the wings, you can either toss them in the sauce or serve the sauce on the side for dipping.
7. **Serve:**
       - Arrange the wings on a serving platter. Serve hot with celery and carrot sticks, and a side of blue cheese or ranch dressing for dipping.

**Tips:**

- **Crispiness:** Baking the wings on a wire rack helps them crisp up better by allowing air circulation around the wings.
- **Sauce:** Adjust the amount of hot sauce and butter to your taste. For a milder sauce, use less hot sauce or add more butter.
- **Storage:** Leftover wings can be stored in the refrigerator for up to 3 days. Reheat in the oven to maintain crispiness.

Enjoy your homemade New York-style Buffalo Wings, perfect for game days or any casual gathering!

**Pork Belly Bao Buns**

**Ingredients:**

- **For the Pork Belly:**
    - 1 pound pork belly, skin on
    - 1 tablespoon soy sauce
    - 1 tablespoon hoisin sauce
    - 1 tablespoon rice vinegar
    - 1 tablespoon brown sugar
    - 1 teaspoon five-spice powder
    - 2 cloves garlic, minced
    - 1 teaspoon ginger, minced
    - 1 cup water
- **For the Bao Buns:**
    - 2 cups all-purpose flour
    - 1/4 cup sugar
    - 1 tablespoon baking powder
    - 1/2 teaspoon salt
    - 1/2 cup warm milk (about 110°F or 45°C)
    - 1 tablespoon active dry yeast
    - 2 tablespoons vegetable oil
- **For the Pickled Vegetables:**
    - 1 cup thinly sliced cucumber
    - 1 cup thinly sliced radishes
    - 1/2 cup rice vinegar
    - 1/4 cup sugar
    - 1/4 cup water
    - 1/2 teaspoon salt
- **For Assembly:**
    - 1/4 cup hoisin sauce
    - 1/4 cup mayonnaise (optional)
    - Fresh cilantro leaves (optional)
    - Thinly sliced scallions (optional)

**Instructions:**

1. **Prepare the Pork Belly:**
    - Preheat your oven to 300°F (150°C).
    - Score the skin of the pork belly in a crisscross pattern. This helps the fat render and the skin crisp up.
    - In a small bowl, mix the soy sauce, hoisin sauce, rice vinegar, brown sugar, five-spice powder, minced garlic, and minced ginger.
    - Rub the mixture all over the pork belly, making sure to get it into the score marks.
    - Place the pork belly in a roasting pan, skin side up, and add the water to the pan.
    - Cover the pan with aluminum foil and roast for 2-2.5 hours, or until the pork is tender.

- Remove the foil and increase the oven temperature to 425°F (220°C). Roast for an additional 20-30 minutes, or until the skin is crispy.
- Let the pork belly rest for about 10 minutes before slicing into bite-sized pieces.

2. **Prepare the Bao Buns:**
   - In a small bowl, dissolve the sugar in the warm milk. Sprinkle the yeast over the top and let it sit for about 5 minutes, or until frothy.
   - In a large bowl, combine the flour, baking powder, and salt. Make a well in the center and pour in the yeast mixture and vegetable oil.
   - Mix until a dough forms. Turn the dough out onto a floured surface and knead for about 5 minutes, or until smooth.
   - Place the dough in a lightly oiled bowl, cover with a damp cloth, and let it rise in a warm place for about 1 hour, or until doubled in size.
   - Punch down the dough and divide it into 12 equal pieces. Roll each piece into a ball and then flatten into a round about 4 inches in diameter.
   - Place each round on a small piece of parchment paper.
   - Steam the buns in a bamboo steamer or a steamer basket lined with parchment paper over boiling water for about 10 minutes, or until puffed and cooked through.

3. **Prepare the Pickled Vegetables:**
   - In a small bowl, combine the rice vinegar, sugar, water, and salt. Stir until the sugar and salt are dissolved.
   - Add the sliced cucumber and radishes to the bowl and let them pickle for at least 15 minutes.

4. **Assemble the Bao Buns:**
   - Spread a little hoisin sauce (and mayonnaise, if using) inside each steamed bao bun.
   - Add a few pieces of pork belly to each bun.
   - Top with pickled vegetables, fresh cilantro leaves, and sliced scallions if desired.

5. **Serve:**
   - Serve the pork belly bao buns warm and enjoy!

**Tips:**

- **Crispy Pork Belly:** For extra crispy skin, you can broil the pork belly for a few minutes after roasting, keeping a close eye to prevent burning.
- **Bao Dough:** If you don't have a steamer, you can use a large pot with a metal rack or heatproof plate over a pot of boiling water.
- **Pickling:** Adjust the pickling time to your taste; longer pickling will result in more tangy vegetables.

These Pork Belly Bao Buns make for a delicious appetizer or a fun meal, bringing a taste of Asian street food to your kitchen!

**Beef Stroganoff**

**Ingredients:**

- **For the Beef:**
    - 1 pound beef sirloin or tenderloin, cut into thin strips
    - 2 tablespoons vegetable oil or butter
    - Salt and freshly ground black pepper, to taste
- **For the Sauce:**
    - 1 medium onion, finely chopped
    - 2 cloves garlic, minced
    - 8 ounces mushrooms, sliced (button or cremini mushrooms work well)
    - 1 tablespoon all-purpose flour
    - 1 cup beef broth
    - 1 tablespoon Worcestershire sauce
    - 1 teaspoon Dijon mustard
    - 1/2 cup sour cream
    - 1 tablespoon chopped fresh parsley (for garnish)
- **For Serving:**
    - 12 ounces egg noodles, cooked according to package instructions
    - Additional chopped fresh parsley (for garnish, optional)

**Instructions:**

1. **Prepare the Beef:**
    - Season the beef strips with salt and pepper.
    - Heat the vegetable oil or butter in a large skillet over medium-high heat. Add the beef strips in batches, making sure not to overcrowd the pan. Sear until browned on all sides, about 2-3 minutes per side. Remove the beef from the skillet and set aside.
2. **Cook the Vegetables:**
    - In the same skillet, add a bit more oil or butter if needed. Add the chopped onion and cook until softened, about 3-4 minutes.
    - Add the minced garlic and cook for an additional 1 minute.
    - Add the sliced mushrooms and cook until they release their moisture and become golden brown, about 5-7 minutes.
3. **Make the Sauce:**
    - Sprinkle the flour over the mushroom mixture and stir to combine. Cook for about 1 minute to eliminate the raw flour taste.
    - Gradually add the beef broth, stirring constantly to avoid lumps. Bring the mixture to a simmer.
    - Stir in the Worcestershire sauce and Dijon mustard. Let the sauce simmer for 5 minutes, or until it thickens slightly.
4. **Finish the Dish:**
    - Reduce the heat to low and stir in the sour cream until well combined. Do not allow the sauce to boil after adding the sour cream to prevent curdling.

- Return the seared beef along with any accumulated juices to the skillet. Stir to combine and heat through, about 2-3 minutes.
5. **Serve:**
    - Serve the beef stroganoff over the cooked egg noodles or rice.
    - Garnish with chopped fresh parsley if desired.

**Tips:**

- **Beef Choice:** For the most tender results, use tender cuts like sirloin, tenderloin, or even ribeye. Avoid overcooking the beef to keep it tender.
- **Sour Cream Substitute:** If you don't have sour cream, you can use Greek yogurt or heavy cream as a substitute.
- **Mushrooms:** If you prefer a different type of mushroom, such as shiitake or porcini, feel free to use them for additional flavor.

Enjoy your homemade Beef Stroganoff, a rich and comforting dish that's perfect for a satisfying meal!

**Lobster Mac and Cheese**

**Ingredients:**

- **For the Mac and Cheese:**
    - 8 ounces elbow macaroni or cavatappi pasta
    - 2 tablespoons unsalted butter
    - 2 tablespoons all-purpose flour
    - 2 cups milk (whole milk is best)
    - 1 cup heavy cream
    - 2 cups shredded sharp cheddar cheese
    - 1 cup shredded Gruyère cheese
    - 1/2 teaspoon Dijon mustard
    - 1/4 teaspoon paprika
    - 1/4 teaspoon garlic powder
    - Salt and freshly ground black pepper, to taste
- **For the Lobster:**
    - 1 pound lobster meat, cooked and chopped (you can use claw and knuckle meat)
    - 1 tablespoon butter (for sautéing)
- **For the Topping (optional):**
    - 1/2 cup panko breadcrumbs
    - 2 tablespoons melted butter
    - 1/4 cup grated Parmesan cheese

**Instructions:**

1. **Cook the Pasta:**
    - Bring a large pot of salted water to a boil. Add the pasta and cook according to package instructions until al dente. Drain and set aside.
2. **Prepare the Cheese Sauce:**
    - In a large saucepan, melt the butter over medium heat.
    - Stir in the flour and cook for about 1-2 minutes, or until the mixture is lightly golden and bubbling. This forms a roux.
    - Gradually whisk in the milk and heavy cream. Continue whisking until the mixture is smooth and begins to thicken, about 5-7 minutes.
    - Reduce the heat to low and stir in the shredded cheddar and Gruyère cheeses until melted and smooth.
    - Add the Dijon mustard, paprika, garlic powder, salt, and black pepper. Adjust seasoning to taste.
3. **Prepare the Lobster:**
    - In a separate skillet, melt 1 tablespoon of butter over medium heat.
    - Add the chopped lobster meat and sauté for about 2-3 minutes, just until warmed through. Be careful not to overcook. Remove from heat and set aside.
4. **Combine and Bake:**
    - Preheat your oven to 375°F (190°C).
    - Add the cooked pasta to the cheese sauce and stir to combine.
    - Gently fold in the sautéed lobster meat.

- Pour the mac and cheese mixture into a greased baking dish.
5. **Prepare the Topping (if using):**
    - In a small bowl, mix together the panko breadcrumbs, melted butter, and grated Parmesan cheese.
    - Sprinkle the breadcrumb mixture evenly over the mac and cheese.
6. **Bake:**
    - Bake in the preheated oven for 20-25 minutes, or until the top is golden brown and the cheese sauce is bubbly.
7. **Serve:**
    - Let the Lobster Mac and Cheese cool for a few minutes before serving. Enjoy it as a luxurious main course or a decadent side dish!

**Tips:**

- **Lobster Meat:** If using pre-cooked lobster meat, ensure it's not overcooked. Fresh or frozen lobster meat can be used, but it should be cooked before adding to the mac and cheese.
- **Cheese:** Feel free to experiment with other cheeses like fontina or provolone for different flavor profiles.
- **Make-Ahead:** You can prepare the mac and cheese ahead of time and store it in the refrigerator. Reheat in the oven until hot and bubbly.

This Lobster Mac and Cheese is a rich and comforting dish that combines the creamy goodness of mac and cheese with the luxurious taste of lobster. Enjoy!

**NYC-style Chicken Parmesan**

**Ingredients:**

- **For the Chicken:**
    - 4 boneless, skinless chicken breasts
    - Salt and freshly ground black pepper, to taste
    - 1 cup all-purpose flour
    - 2 large eggs
    - 1/4 cup milk
    - 1 1/2 cups Italian-style breadcrumbs
    - 1/2 cup grated Parmesan cheese
    - 1 cup marinara sauce
    - 1 1/2 cups shredded mozzarella cheese
    - 1/4 cup chopped fresh basil (optional, for garnish)
    - Olive oil, for frying
- **For Serving:**
    - Cooked spaghetti or other pasta
    - Additional marinara sauce

**Instructions:**

1. **Prepare the Chicken:**
    - Place the chicken breasts between two pieces of plastic wrap or parchment paper. Using a meat mallet or rolling pin, pound the chicken breasts to an even thickness, about 1/2 inch thick. This ensures they cook evenly.
    - Season both sides of the chicken breasts with salt and pepper.
2. **Bread the Chicken:**
    - Set up a breading station: Place the flour in a shallow dish. In another dish, whisk together the eggs and milk. In a third dish, combine the breadcrumbs and grated Parmesan cheese.
    - Dredge each chicken breast in the flour, shaking off any excess. Dip into the egg mixture, then coat evenly with the breadcrumb mixture, pressing gently to adhere.
3. **Fry the Chicken:**
    - Heat about 1/4 inch of olive oil in a large skillet over medium-high heat.
    - Fry the chicken breasts in batches, cooking until golden brown and crispy, about 3-4 minutes per side. The internal temperature of the chicken should reach 165°F (74°C). Transfer the cooked chicken to a paper towel-lined plate to drain excess oil.
4. **Assemble the Chicken Parmesan:**
    - Preheat your oven to 400°F (200°C).
    - Place the fried chicken breasts in a baking dish. Spoon about 2 tablespoons of marinara sauce over each piece of chicken.
    - Sprinkle the shredded mozzarella cheese evenly over the chicken.
5. **Bake:**

- Bake in the preheated oven for 10-15 minutes, or until the cheese is melted and bubbly. If you like a slightly crispy top, you can broil the chicken for an additional 2-3 minutes, keeping a close eye to avoid burning.
6. **Serve:**
    - Garnish with chopped fresh basil, if desired.
    - Serve the Chicken Parmesan over cooked spaghetti or your favorite pasta, with additional marinara sauce on the side.

**Tips:**

- **Chicken:** For an extra crispy coating, you can double-dip the chicken by dipping it back into the egg mixture and breadcrumbs before frying.
- **Cheese:** For a richer flavor, use a combination of mozzarella and provolone cheese.
- **Make-Ahead:** The breaded chicken can be prepared ahead of time and frozen. Reheat and top with sauce and cheese when ready to bake.

Enjoy your NYC-style Chicken Parmesan, a comforting and satisfying dish that brings the classic flavors of Italian-American cuisine right to your table!

# Cinnamon Sugar Donuts

## Ingredients:

- **For the Donuts:**
    - 2 cups all-purpose flour
    - 1 cup granulated sugar
    - 2 teaspoons baking powder
    - 1/2 teaspoon baking soda
    - 1/2 teaspoon salt
    - 1/2 teaspoon ground cinnamon
    - 1/4 teaspoon ground nutmeg (optional)
    - 1/2 cup whole milk
    - 1/4 cup sour cream
    - 2 large eggs
    - 4 tablespoons unsalted butter, melted
    - 1 teaspoon vanilla extract
- **For the Cinnamon Sugar Coating:**
    - 1/2 cup granulated sugar
    - 1 tablespoon ground cinnamon
    - 1/4 cup unsalted butter, melted

## Instructions:

1. **Prepare the Donut Batter:**
    - Preheat your oven to 375°F (190°C). Grease a donut pan or lightly spray it with non-stick cooking spray.
    - In a large bowl, whisk together the flour, sugar, baking powder, baking soda, salt, cinnamon, and nutmeg (if using).
    - In another bowl, combine the milk, sour cream, eggs, melted butter, and vanilla extract.
    - Pour the wet ingredients into the dry ingredients and stir until just combined. The batter will be thick.
2. **Fill the Donut Pan:**
    - Spoon the batter into the donut pan, filling each cavity about 2/3 full. You can also use a piping bag or a zip-top bag with the corner cut off to make this process easier.
3. **Bake the Donuts:**
    - Bake in the preheated oven for 12-15 minutes, or until a toothpick inserted into the center of a donut comes out clean.
    - Allow the donuts to cool in the pan for a few minutes, then transfer them to a wire rack to cool completely.
4. **Prepare the Cinnamon Sugar Coating:**
    - In a small bowl, mix together the sugar and cinnamon.

- Brush the cooled donuts with the melted butter, then dip them in the cinnamon sugar mixture, ensuring they are well coated.
5. **Serve:**
    - Enjoy the donuts fresh and warm. They are best eaten the day they are made but can be stored in an airtight container for up to 2 days.

**Tips:**

- **Frying Option:** If you prefer fried donuts, you can use this recipe for a donut dough, cut out donut shapes, and fry them in hot oil (around 350°F or 175°C) until golden brown. After frying, coat them with cinnamon sugar.
- **Donut Variations:** For a different twist, you can add chocolate chips to the batter or glaze the donuts instead of rolling them in cinnamon sugar.
- **Storage:** To keep them fresh longer, you can freeze the donuts. Just warm them up in the oven for a few minutes before serving.

Enjoy your homemade Cinnamon Sugar Donuts, a perfect blend of sweetness and spice that will make any morning special!

# Classic NY Style Eggplant Rollatini

**Ingredients:**

- **For the Eggplant:**
    - 2 large eggplants
    - Salt, for sprinkling
- **For the Filling:**
    - 1 cup ricotta cheese
    - 1 cup shredded mozzarella cheese
    - 1/2 cup grated Parmesan cheese
    - 1 large egg
    - 1/4 cup chopped fresh basil (or 1 tablespoon dried basil)
    - 1/4 cup chopped fresh parsley
    - 1/2 teaspoon garlic powder
    - Salt and freshly ground black pepper, to taste
- **For the Assembly:**
    - 2 cups marinara sauce (store-bought or homemade)
    - 1 cup shredded mozzarella cheese
    - Fresh basil or parsley, for garnish (optional)

**Instructions:**

1. **Prepare the Eggplant:**
    - Preheat your oven to 375°F (190°C).
    - Slice the eggplants lengthwise into 1/4-inch thick slices. If you prefer, you can peel them partially for a more refined texture.
    - Arrange the eggplant slices in a single layer on a baking sheet. Sprinkle both sides with salt and let them sit for about 30 minutes to draw out excess moisture. This also helps to reduce bitterness.
    - Rinse the eggplant slices under cold water and pat them dry with paper towels.
2. **Roast the Eggplant:**
    - Brush the eggplant slices lightly with olive oil on both sides.
    - Arrange them in a single layer on the baking sheet.
    - Roast in the preheated oven for 20-25 minutes, or until the eggplant is tender and slightly golden. Turn the slices halfway through the cooking time for even roasting.
3. **Prepare the Filling:**
    - In a medium bowl, combine the ricotta cheese, shredded mozzarella, grated Parmesan, egg, chopped basil, chopped parsley, garlic powder, salt, and pepper. Mix until well combined.
4. **Assemble the Rollatini:**
    - Spread a thin layer of marinara sauce on the bottom of a 9x13-inch baking dish.

- Take one roasted eggplant slice and place a spoonful of the ricotta mixture at one end. Roll the eggplant slice around the filling and place it seam-side down in the prepared baking dish. Repeat with the remaining eggplant slices and filling.
- Pour the remaining marinara sauce over the eggplant rolls and sprinkle with the shredded mozzarella cheese.

5. **Bake:**
   - Cover the baking dish with aluminum foil and bake in the preheated oven for 25 minutes.
   - Remove the foil and bake for an additional 10-15 minutes, or until the cheese is melted and bubbly and the top is lightly browned.

6. **Serve:**
   - Let the Eggplant Rollatini cool for a few minutes before serving.
   - Garnish with fresh basil or parsley if desired.

**Tips:**

- **Eggplant Preparation:** Salting the eggplant helps to remove excess moisture and bitterness, but make sure to rinse and dry them thoroughly to avoid a salty dish.
- **Cheese Variations:** You can experiment with other cheeses like fontina or provolone for different flavor profiles.
- **Make-Ahead:** You can assemble the rollatini ahead of time and refrigerate it. Bake it just before serving, adding a few extra minutes to the baking time if it's cold from the fridge.

Enjoy your Classic NY Style Eggplant Rollatini, a flavorful and comforting dish that's sure to impress!

**Stuffed Artichokes**

**Ingredients:**

- **For the Artichokes:**
    - 4 large artichokes
    - 1 lemon, cut in half
    - 2 tablespoons olive oil
    - 2 cloves garlic, minced
- **For the Stuffing:**
    - 1 cup fresh breadcrumbs (preferably from Italian or French bread)
    - 1/2 cup grated Parmesan cheese
    - 1/4 cup chopped fresh parsley (or 2 tablespoons dried parsley)
    - 1 tablespoon chopped fresh basil (or 1 teaspoon dried basil)
    - 1 teaspoon dried oregano
    - 1/4 teaspoon red pepper flakes (optional, for a bit of heat)
    - 2 cloves garlic, minced
    - 1/4 cup olive oil
    - Salt and freshly ground black pepper, to taste

**Instructions:**

1. **Prepare the Artichokes:**
    - Fill a large bowl with water and add the juice of half the lemon.
    - Trim the artichokes: Cut off the top third of each artichoke. Use kitchen shears to snip the sharp tips off the remaining leaves. Cut the stems to about 1 inch long. Remove any small or tough outer leaves.
    - Rub the cut edges of the artichokes with the remaining lemon half to prevent browning.
    - Place the artichokes in the lemon water as you work to keep them from browning.
2. **Pre-cook the Artichokes:**
    - Bring a large pot of salted water to a boil. Add the artichokes and cook for about 10-15 minutes, or until the outer leaves are tender and the artichokes can be pulled off easily.
    - Remove the artichokes from the pot and let them cool slightly.
3. **Prepare the Stuffing:**
    - In a medium bowl, combine the fresh breadcrumbs, grated Parmesan cheese, chopped parsley, chopped basil, dried oregano, red pepper flakes (if using), minced garlic, olive oil, salt, and pepper. Mix until well combined.
4. **Stuff the Artichokes:**
    - Gently pull the outer leaves of each artichoke apart to create space for the stuffing. Using a spoon or your fingers, carefully remove the small, fuzzy choke in the center of the artichoke, exposing the heart.
    - Spoon the stuffing mixture into the spaces between the leaves and into the center of each artichoke. Press down gently to pack the stuffing in.

5. **Bake:**
    - Preheat your oven to 375°F (190°C).
    - Place the stuffed artichokes in a baking dish. Drizzle with olive oil and sprinkle with a bit more salt and pepper.
    - Cover the baking dish with aluminum foil and bake in the preheated oven for 30-40 minutes, or until the artichokes are tender and the stuffing is golden brown. Remove the foil for the last 10 minutes of baking to allow the tops to crisp up.
6. **Serve:**
    - Let the stuffed artichokes cool slightly before serving.
    - Serve warm or at room temperature, with extra lemon wedges if desired.

**Tips:**

- **Cleaning Artichokes:** Be sure to remove all the fuzzy choke from the center of the artichoke. This can be done using a spoon or a melon baller.
- **Breadcrumbs:** Fresh breadcrumbs work best for stuffing, but you can use dried breadcrumbs if necessary. Just add a bit more olive oil to keep the stuffing moist.
- **Variations:** You can add cooked crumbled sausage or chopped nuts to the stuffing for extra flavor and texture.

Enjoy your Stuffed Artichokes, a delicious and elegant dish that's sure to impress!

**Pastry Cream-filled Eclairs**

**Ingredients:**

- **For the Choux Pastry:**
    - 1/2 cup (1 stick) unsalted butter
    - 1 cup water
    - 1/4 teaspoon salt
    - 1 cup all-purpose flour
    - 4 large eggs
- **For the Pastry Cream:**
    - 2 cups whole milk
    - 1/2 cup granulated sugar
    - 1/4 cup cornstarch
    - 4 large egg yolks
    - 4 tablespoons unsalted butter
    - 1 tablespoon vanilla extract
- **For the Chocolate Glaze:**
    - 1/2 cup heavy cream
    - 4 ounces semisweet chocolate, chopped
    - 1 tablespoon light corn syrup (optional, for shine)

**Instructions:**

**1. Prepare the Choux Pastry:**

1. **Preheat the Oven:**
    - Preheat your oven to 375°F (190°C). Line a baking sheet with parchment paper or a silicone baking mat.
2. **Cook the Pastry Base:**
    - In a medium saucepan, combine the butter, water, and salt. Bring to a boil over medium heat, stirring occasionally.
    - Once the butter is melted and the mixture is boiling, remove from heat and quickly add the flour all at once. Stir vigorously with a wooden spoon or spatula until the mixture forms a smooth dough and pulls away from the sides of the pan.
3. **Incorporate the Eggs:**
    - Transfer the dough to a mixing bowl and let it cool for about 5 minutes.
    - Add the eggs one at a time, beating well after each addition until the dough is smooth and glossy. You can use a hand mixer or stand mixer for this step.
4. **Pipe the Eclairs:**
    - Transfer the choux pastry dough to a piping bag fitted with a large round or star tip.
    - Pipe 4-5 inch long strips of dough onto the prepared baking sheet, spacing them about 2 inches apart.
5. **Bake:**

- Bake in the preheated oven for 20-25 minutes, or until the eclairs are golden brown and puffed. Do not open the oven door during the first 15 minutes of baking to prevent them from collapsing.
- Turn off the oven and let the eclairs cool in the oven with the door slightly ajar for 10 minutes. Then transfer to a wire rack to cool completely.

## 2. Prepare the Pastry Cream:

1. **Heat the Milk:**
   - In a medium saucepan, heat the milk over medium heat until it starts to simmer. Remove from heat.
2. **Mix the Egg Yolks and Sugar:**
   - In a separate bowl, whisk together the sugar and cornstarch. Add the egg yolks and whisk until smooth.
3. **Temper the Egg Mixture:**
   - Gradually whisk the hot milk into the egg yolk mixture to temper the eggs and prevent curdling.
4. **Cook the Pastry Cream:**
   - Return the mixture to the saucepan and cook over medium heat, whisking constantly, until the cream thickens and starts to bubble. This should take about 3-5 minutes.
5. **Finish the Cream:**
   - Remove from heat and stir in the butter and vanilla extract until fully combined and smooth.
   - Transfer the pastry cream to a bowl, cover with plastic wrap (pressing the wrap directly onto the surface of the cream to prevent a skin from forming), and refrigerate until cool and set, about 1-2 hours.

## 3. Prepare the Chocolate Glaze:

1. **Heat the Cream:**
   - In a small saucepan, heat the heavy cream over medium heat until it begins to simmer.
2. **Melt the Chocolate:**
   - Place the chopped chocolate in a heatproof bowl. Pour the hot cream over the chocolate and let it sit for a minute. Stir until the chocolate is fully melted and the mixture is smooth.
   - If using, stir in the corn syrup for extra shine.

## 4. Assemble the Eclairs:

1. **Fill the Eclairs:**
   - Once the eclairs are completely cooled, use a small serrated knife to make a slit on one side or the end of each eclair to create an opening.

- Fill a piping bag fitted with a small round tip with the pastry cream. Pipe the cream into the eclairs through the slit until filled.
2. **Glaze the Eclairs:**
   - Dip the top of each filled eclair into the chocolate glaze, or spoon the glaze over the eclairs.
   - Allow the glaze to set before serving.

**Tips:**

- **Choux Pastry:** Ensure your dough is smooth and not too thick. If it's too thick, your eclairs may not puff properly.
- **Piping:** To ensure even eclairs, try to pipe them in the same size and shape.
- **Pastry Cream:** If you find lumps in the pastry cream, you can strain it through a fine mesh sieve before cooling.

Enjoy your homemade Pastry Cream-filled Eclairs—a decadent and delicious treat that's sure to impress!

## Hot Pastrami on Rye

**Ingredients:**

- **For the Sandwich:**
    - 8 slices of rye bread (preferably with caraway seeds)
    - 1 pound hot pastrami, sliced (you can buy pre-sliced or slice it yourself if you have a whole piece)
    - 4 tablespoons yellow mustard (or more, to taste)
    - 4 slices of Swiss cheese (optional, for added flavor)
    - Pickles, for serving (optional)
- **For the Preparation:**
    - 2 tablespoons unsalted butter (for toasting the bread)
    - 1 medium onion, thinly sliced (optional, for caramelizing)

**Instructions:**

1. **Prepare the Pastrami:**
    - If the pastrami is cold, you may want to warm it up. Heat a skillet over medium heat and add the pastrami. Cook for a few minutes, stirring occasionally, until heated through. You can also warm it in the oven by placing it on a baking sheet at 350°F (175°C) for about 10 minutes.
2. **Optional Caramelized Onions:**
    - If you want to add caramelized onions, heat a small amount of oil or butter in a skillet over medium heat. Add the sliced onions and cook, stirring occasionally, until they are golden brown and caramelized, about 15-20 minutes.
3. **Toast the Bread:**
    - Spread a thin layer of butter on one side of each slice of rye bread.
    - Heat a skillet or griddle over medium heat. Place the bread slices, butter-side down, on the skillet. Cook until the bread is golden brown and crispy, about 2-3 minutes per side. Remove from heat and set aside.
4. **Assemble the Sandwich:**
    - Spread a generous amount of mustard on the non-buttered side of 4 slices of rye bread.
    - Layer the warm pastrami evenly over the mustard-covered bread.
    - If using Swiss cheese, place a slice of cheese on top of the pastrami.
    - Optionally, add caramelized onions on top of the pastrami.
    - Top with the remaining slices of rye bread, mustard-side down.
5. **Heat the Sandwich:**
    - To ensure the cheese melts and the sandwich is heated through, you can grill the assembled sandwiches. Heat a skillet or griddle over medium heat. Place the sandwiches on the skillet and press down gently with a spatula. Cook until the bread is golden brown and the cheese is melted, about 2-3 minutes per side.
6. **Serve:**
    - Slice the sandwiches in half, if desired.

- Serve with pickles on the side.

**Tips:**

- **Quality Ingredients:** Use high-quality pastrami and rye bread for the best flavor. If you can get fresh pastrami from a deli, that's ideal.
- **Mustard:** You can adjust the amount of mustard according to your taste. Some people prefer a more generous spread, while others like it light.
- **Cheese:** Swiss cheese is traditional, but you can use other cheeses if you prefer.

Enjoy your Hot Pastrami on Rye—a classic deli sandwich that's sure to satisfy your cravings for something hearty and delicious!

# New York-style Frittata

## Ingredients:

- **For the Frittata:**
    - 8 large eggs
    - 1/2 cup milk or heavy cream
    - 1 cup shredded cheddar cheese (or a mix of your favorite cheeses, like Swiss or mozzarella)
    - 1 cup cooked and crumbled breakfast sausage (optional)
    - 1 medium onion, diced
    - 1 bell pepper (red, green, or yellow), diced
    - 1 cup fresh spinach, chopped
    - 1/2 cup cherry tomatoes, halved
    - 2 cloves garlic, minced
    - 2 tablespoons olive oil
    - Salt and freshly ground black pepper, to taste
    - 1/2 teaspoon dried oregano (optional)
    - 1/4 teaspoon crushed red pepper flakes (optional, for a bit of heat)
- **For Garnish:**
    - Fresh parsley, chopped (optional)
    - Extra cheese, for topping (optional)

## Instructions:

1. **Preheat the Oven:**
    - Preheat your oven to 375°F (190°C).
2. **Prepare the Ingredients:**
    - In a large bowl, whisk together the eggs, milk or cream, salt, and pepper until well combined. Stir in the shredded cheese.
3. **Cook the Vegetables and Meat:**
    - Heat olive oil in a large, oven-safe skillet over medium heat.
    - Add the diced onion and bell pepper to the skillet. Cook until they begin to soften, about 5 minutes.
    - Add the minced garlic and cook for another minute until fragrant.
    - If using sausage, add it to the skillet and cook until heated through and slightly browned.
    - Stir in the chopped spinach and cherry tomatoes. Cook for another 2-3 minutes until the spinach is wilted and the tomatoes are slightly softened.
4. **Combine and Cook:**
    - Spread the vegetable and sausage mixture evenly in the skillet.
    - Pour the egg mixture over the vegetables and sausage. Gently stir to distribute the ingredients evenly.
    - Allow the frittata to cook on the stovetop over medium heat until the edges begin to set, about 5 minutes.

5. **Transfer to Oven:**
   - Transfer the skillet to the preheated oven. Bake for 15-20 minutes, or until the frittata is fully set in the center and lightly golden on top. A knife inserted into the center should come out clean.
6. **Serve:**
   - Let the frittata cool for a few minutes before slicing.
   - Garnish with chopped fresh parsley and extra cheese if desired.

**Tips:**

- **Customizable:** Feel free to add other vegetables or ingredients according to your preference. Mushrooms, zucchini, and broccoli are great additions.
- **Cheese Choices:** For a different flavor, try using feta, goat cheese, or a blend of cheeses.
- **Serving:** This frittata is great warm or at room temperature, making it perfect for a brunch or a make-ahead meal.

Enjoy your New York-style Frittata, a delicious and satisfying dish that's perfect for any meal of the day!

# Shrimp Scampi

## Ingredients:

- **For the Shrimp:**
    - 1 pound large shrimp (16-20 count), peeled and deveined
    - Salt and freshly ground black pepper, to taste
- **For the Scampi Sauce:**
    - 4 tablespoons unsalted butter
    - 2 tablespoons olive oil
    - 4 cloves garlic, minced
    - 1/4 teaspoon red pepper flakes (optional, for a bit of heat)
    - 1/2 cup dry white wine (such as Sauvignon Blanc or Pinot Grigio) or chicken broth
    - Juice of 1 lemon
    - 1/4 cup chopped fresh parsley
    - 1/4 cup grated Parmesan cheese (optional, for serving)
    - Lemon wedges, for garnish
- **For Serving:**
    - Cooked pasta (such as linguine, spaghetti, or fettuccine)
    - Crusty bread (optional, for dipping)

## Instructions:

1. **Prepare the Shrimp:**
    - Season the shrimp with salt and pepper.
2. **Cook the Shrimp:**
    - Heat the olive oil and 2 tablespoons of butter in a large skillet over medium-high heat.
    - Add the shrimp in a single layer and cook for 2-3 minutes on each side, or until they are pink and opaque. Remove the shrimp from the skillet and set aside.
3. **Make the Scampi Sauce:**
    - In the same skillet, add the remaining 2 tablespoons of butter and the minced garlic. Cook for 1 minute, or until the garlic is fragrant but not browned.
    - Add the red pepper flakes (if using) and cook for an additional 30 seconds.
    - Pour in the white wine (or chicken broth) and lemon juice. Bring to a simmer and cook for 2-3 minutes, or until the sauce has reduced slightly.
4. **Combine Shrimp and Sauce:**
    - Return the cooked shrimp to the skillet and toss to coat with the sauce. Cook for 1-2 minutes, or until the shrimp are heated through and well-coated with the sauce.
    - Stir in the chopped parsley.
5. **Serve:**

- If serving with pasta, toss the cooked pasta in the skillet with the scampi sauce and shrimp, or place the pasta on serving plates and spoon the shrimp and sauce over the top.
        - Sprinkle with grated Parmesan cheese if desired and garnish with lemon wedges.
6. **Optional:**
    - Serve with crusty bread for dipping into the delicious sauce.

**Tips:**

- **Shrimp Size:** Large shrimp are best for this recipe, but you can use smaller shrimp if you prefer. Adjust the cooking time accordingly.
- **Wine Substitute:** If you don't have white wine, you can use chicken broth or even a splash of lemon juice as a substitute.
- **Garlic:** Be careful not to overcook the garlic, as it can become bitter if browned too much.

Enjoy your Shrimp Scampi, a simple yet elegant dish that's perfect for a quick weeknight dinner or a special occasion!

**Classic NYC Meatballs**

**Ingredients:**

- **For the Meatballs:**
    - 1 pound ground beef (80% lean)
    - 1/2 pound ground pork
    - 1 cup fresh breadcrumbs (preferably from Italian or French bread)
    - 1/4 cup grated Parmesan cheese
    - 1/4 cup chopped fresh parsley
    - 2 large eggs
    - 3 cloves garlic, minced
    - 1/2 cup milk
    - 1 teaspoon dried oregano
    - 1/2 teaspoon dried basil
    - 1/4 teaspoon red pepper flakes (optional, for a bit of heat)
    - Salt and freshly ground black pepper, to taste
- **For the Tomato Sauce (optional, but recommended):**
    - 2 cups marinara sauce or homemade tomato sauce
    - 1 tablespoon olive oil
    - 1/2 onion, finely chopped
    - 2 cloves garlic, minced
    - 1/2 teaspoon dried oregano
    - 1/2 teaspoon dried basil
    - Salt and freshly ground black pepper, to taste

**Instructions:**

1. **Prepare the Meatball Mixture:**
    - Preheat your oven to 375°F (190°C).
    - In a large bowl, combine the ground beef and ground pork.
    - Add the breadcrumbs, Parmesan cheese, parsley, eggs, minced garlic, milk, oregano, basil, red pepper flakes (if using), salt, and pepper. Mix gently until everything is well combined. Avoid over-mixing to keep the meatballs tender.
2. **Form the Meatballs:**
    - Shape the mixture into meatballs about 1.5 inches in diameter. Place them on a baking sheet lined with parchment paper or lightly greased.
3. **Bake the Meatballs:**
    - Bake in the preheated oven for 20-25 minutes, or until the meatballs are browned and cooked through. The internal temperature should be 160°F (71°C).
4. **Prepare the Tomato Sauce (if using):**
    - While the meatballs are baking, heat olive oil in a large skillet over medium heat.
    - Add the finely chopped onion and cook until softened, about 5 minutes.
    - Add the minced garlic and cook for another minute until fragrant.

- Stir in the marinara sauce, dried oregano, dried basil, salt, and pepper. Bring to a simmer and cook for 10 minutes to let the flavors meld.
5. **Combine Meatballs and Sauce:**
    - Once the meatballs are baked, add them to the simmering tomato sauce. Let them cook together for an additional 10 minutes, allowing the meatballs to absorb the flavors of the sauce.
6. **Serve:**
    - Serve the meatballs with pasta, in a sub roll for a meatball sandwich, or with a side of crusty bread. Garnish with extra Parmesan cheese and fresh parsley if desired.

**Tips:**

- **Breadcrumbs:** Use fresh breadcrumbs for the best texture. If using store-bought, make sure they are not too dry.
- **Meat Mix:** Combining beef and pork gives the meatballs a nice balance of flavor and fat. You can adjust the ratio based on your preference.
- **Sauce Enhancement:** If using store-bought marinara sauce, you can enhance its flavor with additional herbs or a splash of red wine.

Enjoy your Classic NYC Meatballs, a delicious and hearty dish that's sure to satisfy!

Fresh Ricotta with Honey

**Ingredients:**

- 1 cup fresh ricotta cheese (store-bought or homemade)
- 2-3 tablespoons honey (adjust to taste)
- Fresh fruit or berries (such as strawberries, blueberries, or figs), for garnish (optional)
- Fresh mint leaves, for garnish (optional)
- Toasted bread or crackers (optional, for serving)

**Instructions:**

1. **Prepare the Ricotta:**
    - If you're using store-bought ricotta, spoon it into a serving dish. If you're making homemade ricotta, let it cool to room temperature before serving.
2. **Drizzle with Honey:**
    - Drizzle honey generously over the ricotta cheese. You can adjust the amount of honey based on your sweetness preference.
3. **Garnish (Optional):**
    - If using fresh fruit or berries, arrange them around or on top of the ricotta. Fresh mint leaves can also be added for a touch of color and flavor.
4. **Serve:**
    - Serve immediately with toasted bread or crackers, if desired. The bread or crackers provide a nice contrast to the creamy ricotta and sweet honey.

**Tips:**

- **Ricotta Quality:** For the best flavor, use high-quality fresh ricotta. Homemade ricotta, if you have the time, will be even more flavorful.
- **Honey Varieties:** Try different types of honey (such as clover, wildflower, or lavender) to add unique flavors.
- **Seasonal Fruit:** Depending on the season, you can use different fruits for garnish. Fresh figs, sliced peaches, or apples also pair well with ricotta and honey.

Enjoy this Fresh Ricotta with Honey as a light and delightful treat that highlights the simple pleasures of quality ingredients!

**New York-style Potato Latkes**

**Ingredients:**

- 4 large russet potatoes, peeled
- 1 medium onion, peeled
- 2 large eggs
- 1/4 cup all-purpose flour (or matzo meal for a more traditional touch)
- 1 teaspoon salt
- 1/2 teaspoon black pepper
- 1/2 teaspoon baking powder (optional, for extra crispiness)
- Vegetable oil or canola oil, for frying

**Instructions:**

1. **Prepare the Potatoes and Onion:**
   - Grate the potatoes and onion using a box grater or food processor. For a finer texture, you can use the grating attachment of the food processor.
   - After grating, place the potatoes and onion in a large bowl of cold water. This helps to remove excess starch and prevents the potatoes from turning brown.
2. **Drain and Dry:**
   - Drain the potato and onion mixture in a colander. Press down with a clean kitchen towel or paper towels to remove as much moisture as possible. The drier the mixture, the crispier the latkes will be.
3. **Mix the Latke Batter:**
   - In a large bowl, beat the eggs and then add the grated potato and onion mixture. Stir in the flour (or matzo meal), salt, pepper, and baking powder (if using).
4. **Heat the Oil:**
   - Heat about 1/4 inch of vegetable oil or canola oil in a large skillet over medium-high heat. To test if the oil is hot enough, drop a small amount of the batter into the oil; it should sizzle and rise to the surface.
5. **Fry the Latkes:**
   - Drop heaping tablespoons of the potato mixture into the hot oil, flattening them slightly with the back of the spoon to form small pancakes.
   - Fry in batches, being careful not to overcrowd the pan. Cook each side for about 3-4 minutes, or until the latkes are golden brown and crispy.
   - Remove the latkes with a slotted spoon and drain them on a plate lined with paper towels to remove excess oil.
6. **Serve:**
   - Serve the latkes hot, with traditional accompaniments like applesauce and sour cream, or with your favorite toppings.

**Tips:**

- **Grating:** For a more uniform texture, make sure to grate the potatoes and onions finely. If you prefer a chunkier texture, you can coarsely grate them.
- **Oil Temperature:** Keeping the oil at the right temperature is crucial for crispy latkes. If the oil is too cool, the latkes will be greasy; if it's too hot, they may burn on the outside before cooking through.
- **Making Ahead:** Latkes are best enjoyed fresh and crispy. If you need to make them ahead of time, you can reheat them in a 375°F (190°C) oven for a few minutes to crisp them up.

Enjoy your New York-style Potato Latkes, a delightful and crispy treat that's perfect for any occasion!

**Coney Island Hot Dogs**

**Ingredients:**

- **For the Hot Dogs:**
    - 8 beef hot dogs
    - 8 hot dog buns
- **For the Coney Island Chili Sauce:**
    - 1 pound ground beef
    - 1 medium onion, finely chopped
    - 2 cloves garlic, minced
    - 1 can (15 ounces) tomato sauce
    - 2 tablespoons tomato paste
    - 1/4 cup beef broth
    - 1 tablespoon chili powder
    - 1 teaspoon ground cumin
    - 1/2 teaspoon paprika
    - 1/2 teaspoon dried oregano
    - 1/4 teaspoon cayenne pepper (optional, for extra heat)
    - 1 tablespoon brown sugar
    - Salt and freshly ground black pepper, to taste
- **For the Toppings:**
    - Yellow mustard
    - Finely chopped onions (optional)
    - Shredded cheddar cheese (optional)

**Instructions:**

1. **Prepare the Chili Sauce:**
    - In a large skillet, cook the ground beef over medium heat until browned, breaking it up with a spoon as it cooks. Drain excess fat if necessary.
    - Add the finely chopped onion and minced garlic to the skillet and cook until the onion is softened, about 5 minutes.
    - Stir in the tomato sauce, tomato paste, and beef broth.
    - Add the chili powder, ground cumin, paprika, dried oregano, cayenne pepper (if using), brown sugar, salt, and pepper. Mix well.
    - Reduce the heat to low and let the sauce simmer for about 20-30 minutes, stirring occasionally, until thickened. Adjust seasoning to taste.
2. **Cook the Hot Dogs:**
    - Grill or boil the hot dogs according to your preference. For grilling, cook over medium heat for about 5-7 minutes, turning occasionally until heated through and slightly charred. For boiling, simmer in water for about 5 minutes.
3. **Assemble the Hot Dogs:**
    - Place each hot dog in a bun.
    - Spoon a generous amount of the Coney Island chili sauce over each hot dog.

- Add a squirt of yellow mustard on top.
- Optionally, sprinkle with finely chopped onions and shredded cheddar cheese if desired.
4. **Serve:**
    - Serve the hot dogs immediately with your favorite sides, like potato chips, fries, or a fresh salad.

**Tips:**

- **Chili Sauce:** You can make the chili sauce ahead of time and store it in the refrigerator for up to a week. Reheat it before serving.
- **Buns:** For extra flavor, toast the hot dog buns lightly on the grill or in a toaster oven.
- **Heat Level:** Adjust the amount of cayenne pepper in the chili sauce to suit your heat preference.

Enjoy your Coney Island Hot Dogs, a delicious and nostalgic treat that brings a taste of classic American street food right to your kitchen!

**New York-style Beef Brisket**

**Ingredients:**

- **For the Brisket:**
    - 4-5 pounds beef brisket (whole, untrimmed or trimmed according to preference)
    - 2 tablespoons vegetable oil
    - 1 large onion, chopped
    - 4 cloves garlic, minced
    - 2 cups beef broth
    - 1 cup dry red wine (optional, or use additional beef broth)
    - 2 tablespoons tomato paste
    - 1 tablespoon Worcestershire sauce
    - 1 tablespoon soy sauce
    - 2 teaspoons dried thyme
    - 1 teaspoon dried rosemary
    - 2 bay leaves
    - Salt and freshly ground black pepper, to taste
- **For the Rub:**
    - 2 tablespoons brown sugar
    - 1 tablespoon paprika
    - 1 tablespoon garlic powder
    - 1 tablespoon onion powder
    - 1 teaspoon smoked paprika (optional, for extra smokiness)
    - 1 teaspoon ground cumin
    - 1 teaspoon black pepper
    - 1 teaspoon salt

**Instructions:**

1. **Prepare the Rub:**
    - In a small bowl, combine the brown sugar, paprika, garlic powder, onion powder, smoked paprika (if using), ground cumin, black pepper, and salt.
    - Rub the mixture all over the brisket, covering it evenly. Let the brisket sit at room temperature for about 30 minutes to absorb the flavors.
2. **Brown the Brisket:**
    - Heat vegetable oil in a large skillet or Dutch oven over medium-high heat.
    - Sear the brisket on all sides until browned, about 4-5 minutes per side. Transfer the brisket to a plate and set aside.
3. **Sauté Vegetables:**
    - In the same skillet or Dutch oven, add the chopped onion and cook until softened, about 5 minutes.
    - Add the minced garlic and cook for another minute until fragrant.
4. **Deglaze and Make the Braising Liquid:**
    - Stir in the tomato paste and cook for 1-2 minutes.

- Pour in the red wine (if using) and scrape up any browned bits from the bottom of the pan.
- Add the beef broth, Worcestershire sauce, soy sauce, dried thyme, dried rosemary, and bay leaves. Stir to combine.

5. **Braise the Brisket:**
   - Return the browned brisket to the Dutch oven or skillet, making sure it's partially submerged in the liquid.
   - Cover the pot with a lid and transfer it to a preheated oven at 325°F (163°C).
   - Cook for 3-4 hours, or until the brisket is fork-tender and easily shreds. Alternatively, you can braise it on the stovetop over low heat for the same amount of time.

6. **Rest and Slice:**
   - Once the brisket is tender, remove it from the oven and let it rest for 10-15 minutes before slicing.
   - Slice the brisket against the grain into thin slices.

7. **Serve:**
   - Serve the sliced brisket with the braising liquid and vegetables. It pairs wonderfully with mashed potatoes, roasted vegetables, or a side of coleslaw.

**Tips:**

- **Trimming the Brisket:** You can trim excess fat from the brisket before cooking if you prefer. However, some fat adds flavor and moisture during cooking.
- **Resting the Meat:** Allowing the brisket to rest before slicing helps it retain its juices and improves the texture.
- **Leftovers:** The brisket can be refrigerated for up to 5 days or frozen for up to 3 months. Reheat gently to avoid drying it out.

Enjoy your New York-style Beef Brisket, a classic dish that's sure to impress with its rich flavors and tender texture!

# Blackened Salmon

**Ingredients:**

- **For the Salmon:**
    - 4 salmon fillets (about 6 ounces each), skinless and boneless
    - 2 tablespoons olive oil (or melted butter)
- **For the Blackened Seasoning:**
    - 1 tablespoon paprika
    - 1 teaspoon cayenne pepper (adjust to taste for heat)
    - 1 teaspoon garlic powder
    - 1 teaspoon onion powder
    - 1 teaspoon dried oregano
    - 1 teaspoon dried thyme
    - 1/2 teaspoon ground cumin
    - 1/2 teaspoon smoked paprika (optional, for extra smokiness)
    - 1/2 teaspoon black pepper
    - 1/2 teaspoon salt

**Instructions:**

1. **Prepare the Blackened Seasoning:**
    - In a small bowl, combine all the blackened seasoning ingredients. Mix well to combine.
2. **Season the Salmon:**
    - Pat the salmon fillets dry with paper towels. Brush each fillet with olive oil or melted butter.
    - Sprinkle the blackened seasoning evenly over both sides of each salmon fillet, pressing gently to adhere the spices to the fish.
3. **Heat the Pan:**
    - Heat a large skillet or cast-iron pan over medium-high heat. Add a little oil if needed, but be careful not to use too much, as the seasoning can burn if there's excess oil.
4. **Cook the Salmon:**
    - Once the pan is hot, place the seasoned salmon fillets in the pan. Cook for about 3-4 minutes per side, or until the salmon is cooked through and has a blackened crust. The internal temperature should reach 145°F (63°C), and the fish should flake easily with a fork.
5. **Rest and Serve:**
    - Remove the salmon from the pan and let it rest for a few minutes before serving. This allows the juices to redistribute and enhances the flavor.
6. **Serve:**
    - Serve the blackened salmon with your choice of sides, such as roasted vegetables, a fresh salad, or rice. A squeeze of lemon juice over the top can add a nice touch of brightness.

**Tips:**

- **Pan Temperature:** Make sure the pan is very hot before adding the salmon to achieve a good sear and blackened crust.
- **Adjusting Spice Level:** If you prefer a milder flavor, reduce the amount of cayenne pepper in the seasoning.
- **Marinating:** For a more intense flavor, you can marinate the salmon with the seasoning for 30 minutes before cooking, but it's not necessary.

Enjoy your Blackened Salmon, a delicious and aromatic dish with a perfect balance of spice and flavor!

# Classic NYC Meatloaf

## Ingredients:

- **For the Meatloaf:**
    - 1 pound ground beef (80% lean)
    - 1/2 pound ground pork
    - 1 onion, finely chopped
    - 2 cloves garlic, minced
    - 1 cup fresh breadcrumbs (preferably from Italian or French bread)
    - 1/2 cup milk
    - 2 large eggs
    - 1/4 cup ketchup (plus extra for topping)
    - 2 tablespoons Worcestershire sauce
    - 1 teaspoon dried thyme
    - 1 teaspoon dried oregano
    - 1/2 teaspoon dried basil
    - Salt and freshly ground black pepper, to taste
- **For the Glaze:**
    - 1/4 cup ketchup
    - 2 tablespoons brown sugar
    - 1 tablespoon Worcestershire sauce

## Instructions:

1. **Preheat Oven:**
    - Preheat your oven to 350°F (175°C).
2. **Prepare the Meatloaf Mixture:**
    - In a large bowl, combine the ground beef and ground pork.
    - Add the finely chopped onion and minced garlic, mixing until evenly distributed.
    - Stir in the fresh breadcrumbs, milk, eggs, 1/4 cup ketchup, Worcestershire sauce, dried thyme, dried oregano, dried basil, salt, and pepper. Mix gently until just combined. Be careful not to overmix, as this can make the meatloaf tough.
3. **Form the Meatloaf:**
    - Transfer the meat mixture to a baking dish or a rimmed baking sheet. Shape it into a loaf about 9x5 inches in size.
4. **Prepare the Glaze:**
    - In a small bowl, mix together 1/4 cup ketchup, brown sugar, and 1 tablespoon Worcestershire sauce.
    - Spread the glaze evenly over the top of the meatloaf.
5. **Bake the Meatloaf:**
    - Bake in the preheated oven for 1 hour, or until the internal temperature reaches 160°F (71°C) and the meatloaf is cooked through.
6. **Rest and Serve:**

- Let the meatloaf rest for 10 minutes before slicing. This helps the juices redistribute and makes it easier to cut.
7. **Serve:**
    - Slice and serve the meatloaf with your favorite sides, such as mashed potatoes, green beans, or a simple salad.

**Tips:**

- **Meat Combination:** The blend of ground beef and pork gives the meatloaf a good balance of flavor and fat, but you can use all beef if you prefer.
- **Breadcrumbs:** Fresh breadcrumbs give a better texture than dry breadcrumbs. If you only have dry breadcrumbs, you can use them, but you might need to adjust the amount of milk to achieve the right consistency.
- **Make-Ahead:** You can prepare the meatloaf mixture a day in advance and store it in the refrigerator. Add the glaze just before baking.

Enjoy your Classic NYC Meatloaf, a timeless and satisfying dish that's sure to be a hit at any dinner table!

**Bagel with Lox and Cream Cheese**

**Ingredients:**

- **For the Bagel:**
    - 1 fresh bagel (plain, sesame, or poppy seed, according to preference)
- **For the Topping:**
    - 2-3 tablespoons cream cheese (plain or flavored, such as chive)
    - 2-3 ounces lox (smoked salmon)
    - 1/4 red onion, thinly sliced
    - 1-2 tablespoons capers, drained
    - 1 tomato, thinly sliced (optional)
    - Fresh dill, for garnish (optional)
    - Lemon wedges, for serving (optional)
    - Black pepper, to taste

**Instructions:**

1. **Prepare the Bagel:**
    - Slice the bagel in half horizontally. Toast it if desired, to add a bit of crunch and enhance the flavor.
2. **Spread the Cream Cheese:**
    - Generously spread cream cheese over both halves of the toasted bagel. Use a knife or a spreader to evenly coat the bagel.
3. **Add the Lox:**
    - Lay the lox slices over the cream cheese. You can arrange the slices in a single layer or fold them for a more abundant topping.
4. **Add the Garnishes:**
    - Top the lox with thin slices of red onion, capers, and tomato slices if using.
    - Sprinkle fresh dill over the top if you like.
    - Add a few cracks of black pepper to taste.
5. **Serve:**
    - Serve immediately with lemon wedges on the side if desired. A squeeze of lemon juice can add a fresh, zesty flavor to the lox.

**Tips:**

- **Bagel Selection:** The classic choice is a plain bagel, but sesame and poppy seed bagels are also popular and add extra flavor and texture.
- **Cream Cheese Variations:** You can use flavored cream cheeses, such as chive or herb, for added taste.
- **Lox Quality:** Fresh, high-quality lox will enhance the overall flavor of the dish. Look for lox from a reputable deli or specialty store.

Enjoy your Bagel with Lox and Cream Cheese, a delightful and iconic breakfast that captures the essence of New York-style cuisine!

# Sweet and Sour Meatballs

**Ingredients:**

- **For the Meatballs:**
    - 1 pound ground beef (or a mix of beef and pork)
    - 1/2 cup breadcrumbs
    - 1/4 cup grated Parmesan cheese
    - 1/4 cup milk
    - 1 large egg
    - 1/2 onion, finely chopped
    - 2 cloves garlic, minced
    - 1 teaspoon dried oregano
    - 1/2 teaspoon dried basil
    - Salt and freshly ground black pepper, to taste
- **For the Sweet and Sour Sauce:**
    - 1 cup ketchup
    - 1/2 cup brown sugar
    - 1/4 cup white vinegar
    - 2 tablespoons soy sauce
    - 1 tablespoon cornstarch
    - 1/4 cup water
    - 1/2 teaspoon garlic powder (optional, for extra flavor)
    - 1/4 teaspoon onion powder (optional)

**Instructions:**

1. **Preheat Oven:**
    - Preheat your oven to 375°F (190°C).
2. **Prepare the Meatballs:**
    - In a large bowl, combine the ground beef, breadcrumbs, grated Parmesan cheese, milk, egg, finely chopped onion, minced garlic, dried oregano, dried basil, salt, and pepper. Mix until just combined. Avoid overmixing to keep the meatballs tender.
    - Shape the mixture into meatballs, about 1 to 1.5 inches in diameter. Place the meatballs on a baking sheet lined with parchment paper or in a lightly greased baking dish.
3. **Bake the Meatballs:**
    - Bake the meatballs in the preheated oven for 20-25 minutes, or until cooked through and browned on the outside. An internal temperature of 160°F (71°C) indicates they are done.
4. **Prepare the Sweet and Sour Sauce:**
    - In a medium saucepan, combine ketchup, brown sugar, white vinegar, and soy sauce. Stir well.

- In a small bowl, mix the cornstarch with water until smooth, then add to the sauce mixture. This will thicken the sauce.
- Heat the saucepan over medium heat, stirring constantly until the sauce comes to a boil and thickens, about 5-7 minutes. Add garlic powder and onion powder if using.

5. **Combine Meatballs and Sauce:**
    - Once the meatballs are done baking, remove them from the oven.
    - Transfer the meatballs to the saucepan with the sweet and sour sauce, stirring gently to coat them evenly.
6. **Serve:**
    - Serve the meatballs hot, garnished with chopped green onions or sesame seeds if desired. They are great on their own or served with rice or noodles.

**Tips:**

- **Meatball Variations:** You can substitute ground turkey or chicken for a lighter option.
- **Sauce Adjustments:** Adjust the sweetness or sourness of the sauce to taste by varying the amount of sugar or vinegar.
- **Make-Ahead:** You can prepare the meatballs and sauce in advance. Store separately in the refrigerator and combine before serving.

Enjoy your Sweet and Sour Meatballs, a delicious dish that perfectly balances sweet and tangy flavors with savory meatballs!

# Roasted Garlic Mashed Potatoes

## Ingredients:

- **For the Roasted Garlic:**
    - 1 whole head of garlic
    - 1 tablespoon olive oil
    - Salt, to taste
- **For the Mashed Potatoes:**
    - 2 pounds russet or Yukon Gold potatoes, peeled and cut into chunks
    - 1/2 cup milk (whole milk or cream for richer flavor)
    - 1/4 cup unsalted butter
    - 1/2 cup sour cream (optional, for extra creaminess)
    - Salt and freshly ground black pepper, to taste
    - Chopped fresh chives or parsley for garnish (optional)

## Instructions:

1. **Roast the Garlic:**
    - Preheat your oven to 400°F (200°C).
    - Slice off the top of the garlic head to expose the cloves.
    - Drizzle the exposed garlic with olive oil and sprinkle with a pinch of salt.
    - Wrap the garlic head in aluminum foil and place it on a baking sheet.
    - Roast for 35-40 minutes, or until the garlic is soft and caramelized.
    - Let the garlic cool slightly, then squeeze the cloves out of their skins and mash them into a paste. Set aside.
2. **Prepare the Potatoes:**
    - While the garlic is roasting, place the potato chunks in a large pot and cover with cold water.
    - Add a pinch of salt to the water and bring to a boil over medium-high heat.
    - Reduce the heat to a simmer and cook the potatoes for 15-20 minutes, or until they are tender and easily pierced with a fork.
3. **Mash the Potatoes:**
    - Drain the potatoes and return them to the pot or a large mixing bowl.
    - Use a potato masher or a ricer to mash the potatoes until smooth.
4. **Combine Ingredients:**
    - In a small saucepan, heat the milk and butter until the butter is melted and the mixture is warm.
    - Gradually add the warm milk and butter mixture to the mashed potatoes, stirring until creamy and smooth.
    - Fold in the roasted garlic paste.
    - Add sour cream if using, and mix until well combined.
    - Season with salt and freshly ground black pepper to taste.
5. **Serve:**
    - Transfer the mashed potatoes to a serving dish.

- Garnish with chopped fresh chives or parsley if desired.

**Tips:**

- **Texture:** For extra creamy mashed potatoes, you can use a potato ricer or food mill instead of a masher.
- **Make-Ahead:** These mashed potatoes can be made ahead of time. Reheat gently in a covered dish in the oven at 350°F (175°C) for about 20 minutes, adding a splash of milk if needed.
- **Variations:** Add a splash of cream for a richer texture or mix in grated cheese for an extra indulgent dish.

Enjoy your Roasted Garlic Mashed Potatoes, a delicious and aromatic twist on a classic side dish that's perfect for any meal!

# Classic NYC Chicken Soup

**Ingredients:**

- **For the Soup:**
    - 1 whole chicken (about 3-4 pounds), preferably with skin and bones
    - 1 large onion, peeled and halved
    - 2 large carrots, peeled and cut into chunks
    - 2 stalks celery, cut into chunks
    - 3 cloves garlic, peeled and smashed
    - 1-2 bay leaves
    - 1 teaspoon dried thyme
    - 1 teaspoon dried dill (or 1 tablespoon fresh dill, if available)
    - 10-12 cups water
    - Salt and freshly ground black pepper, to taste
- **For the Soup Garnishes:**
    - 2 large carrots, diced
    - 2 stalks celery, diced
    - 1 cup egg noodles or matzo balls (optional, for a heartier soup)
    - Fresh dill or parsley, chopped (for garnish)

**Instructions:**

1. **Prepare the Broth:**
    - Place the whole chicken in a large pot. Add the halved onion, carrot chunks, celery chunks, garlic, bay leaves, dried thyme, and dried dill.
    - Add 10-12 cups of water, or enough to cover the chicken and vegetables.
    - Bring to a boil over medium-high heat. Once boiling, reduce the heat to low and simmer gently, uncovered, for about 1.5 to 2 hours. Skim off any foam or impurities that rise to the surface.
2. **Remove the Chicken:**
    - After simmering, carefully remove the chicken from the pot using tongs or a slotted spoon. Place the chicken on a cutting board and let it cool slightly.
3. **Strain the Broth:**
    - Strain the broth through a fine-mesh sieve or cheesecloth into another large pot or bowl to remove the vegetables and any remaining bones. Discard the solids.
4. **Prepare the Soup:**
    - Return the strained broth to the pot. Add diced carrots and celery. Simmer until the vegetables are tender, about 10-15 minutes.
    - While the vegetables are cooking, shred the chicken meat from the bones, discarding the skin and bones. Add the shredded chicken back into the pot.
5. **Add Noodles or Matzo Balls (if using):**
    - If using egg noodles, add them to the pot and cook according to package instructions, usually about 5-7 minutes, until tender.

- If using matzo balls, prepare them according to package instructions and add them to the soup just before serving.
6. **Season and Serve:**
    - Taste the soup and season with salt and freshly ground black pepper as needed.
    - Garnish with fresh dill or parsley if desired.
7. **Serve:**
    - Ladle the soup into bowls and enjoy with some crusty bread or matzo on the side.

**Tips:**

- **Broth Clarity:** For a clearer broth, you can cool the soup and skim off any fat that solidifies on the surface. Reheat before serving.
- **Make-Ahead:** The soup can be made ahead of time and stored in the refrigerator for up to 3 days or frozen for up to 3 months. Reheat gently before serving.
- **Noodle Alternatives:** If you prefer, you can use rice or other small pasta shapes instead of egg noodles.

Enjoy your Classic NYC Chicken Soup, a timeless and soothing dish that's perfect for any occasion!

## NYC-style Chopped Cheese

**Ingredients:**

- **For the Chopped Cheese:**
    - 1 pound ground beef (80% lean)
    - 1 medium onion, finely chopped
    - 1 bell pepper, finely chopped (optional)
    - 2-3 cloves garlic, minced
    - 2 tablespoons vegetable oil
    - Salt and freshly ground black pepper, to taste
    - 4-6 slices American cheese (or cheddar cheese if preferred)
    - 4 sub rolls or hero rolls (or any hoagie-style bread)
- **For the Toppings:**
    - Lettuce, shredded
    - Tomato, sliced
    - Pickles, sliced
    - Ketchup
    - Mayonnaise
    - Mustard

**Instructions:**

1. **Cook the Beef Mixture:**
    - Heat vegetable oil in a large skillet or griddle over medium-high heat.
    - Add the finely chopped onion (and bell pepper if using) and cook until softened, about 3-4 minutes.
    - Add the minced garlic and cook for an additional minute until fragrant.
    - Add the ground beef to the skillet. Cook, breaking up the beef with a spatula, until it is browned and fully cooked. Season with salt and pepper.
    - Once the beef is browned, continue to cook, occasionally stirring and chopping the beef into small pieces with your spatula to create a "chopped" texture.
2. **Add Cheese:**
    - Lower the heat to medium. Place the cheese slices over the beef mixture. Cover the skillet with a lid or foil to help the cheese melt, about 2-3 minutes.
3. **Prepare the Rolls:**
    - While the cheese is melting, slice the sub rolls in half lengthwise, without cutting all the way through, creating a pocket for the filling.
    - Optionally, you can toast the rolls lightly in a separate skillet or under the broiler for extra crunch.
4. **Assemble the Sandwiches:**
    - Once the cheese is melted and combined with the beef mixture, use a spatula to divide the mixture among the rolls.
    - Add shredded lettuce, tomato slices, and pickles on top of the beef mixture.
    - Spread ketchup, mayonnaise, and mustard on the inside of the rolls to taste.

5. **Serve:**
    - Serve the sandwiches hot, with your favorite sides like fries or chips.

**Tips:**

- **Cheese Variations:** While American cheese is traditional, you can use other cheeses if preferred, such as cheddar or Swiss.
- **Add-Ins:** Customize your chopped cheese with additional ingredients like sautéed mushrooms, hot peppers, or even a fried egg if you like.
- **Meat Options:** For a lighter version, you can use ground turkey or chicken instead of beef, though the flavor will be different.

Enjoy your NYC-style Chopped Cheese, a delicious and classic New York sandwich that's perfect for a satisfying meal!

**New York-style Apple Pie**

**Ingredients:**

- **For the Pie Crust:**
    - 2 1/2 cups all-purpose flour
    - 1 cup (2 sticks) unsalted butter, cold and cut into small cubes
    - 1/4 cup granulated sugar
    - 1/2 teaspoon salt
    - 1/4 to 1/2 cup ice water
- **For the Apple Filling:**
    - 6-8 medium apples (a mix of tart and sweet varieties such as Granny Smith and Honeycrisp), peeled, cored, and sliced
    - 3/4 cup granulated sugar
    - 1/4 cup light brown sugar, packed
    - 2 tablespoons all-purpose flour or cornstarch
    - 1 tablespoon lemon juice
    - 1 teaspoon ground cinnamon
    - 1/4 teaspoon ground nutmeg
    - 1/4 teaspoon ground allspice
    - 1/4 teaspoon salt
- **For the Assembly:**
    - 1 egg, beaten (for egg wash)
    - 1 tablespoon granulated sugar (for sprinkling)

**Instructions:**

1. **Prepare the Pie Crust:**
    - In a large bowl, whisk together the flour, granulated sugar, and salt.
    - Add the cold butter cubes and use a pastry cutter or your fingers to work the butter into the flour mixture until it resembles coarse crumbs with pea-sized pieces of butter.
    - Gradually add ice water, one tablespoon at a time, and mix until the dough just starts to come together. Be careful not to add too much water.
    - Divide the dough in half, shape each half into a disc, and wrap in plastic wrap. Chill in the refrigerator for at least 1 hour.
2. **Prepare the Apple Filling:**
    - In a large bowl, toss the sliced apples with granulated sugar, brown sugar, flour (or cornstarch), lemon juice, cinnamon, nutmeg, allspice, and salt until evenly coated. Set aside.
3. **Assemble the Pie:**
    - Preheat your oven to 425°F (220°C).
    - On a lightly floured surface, roll out one disc of dough to fit a 9-inch pie pan. Transfer the rolled dough to the pie pan, pressing it into the bottom and sides.

- Fill the pie crust with the apple mixture, mounding the apples slightly in the center.
- Roll out the second disc of dough and place it over the apple filling. Trim any excess dough from the edges, then crimp the edges to seal. Cut a few small slits or use a decorative cutter to create vents in the top crust to allow steam to escape.
- Brush the top crust with the beaten egg and sprinkle with granulated sugar.

4. **Bake the Pie:**
   - Place the pie on a baking sheet to catch any drips and bake in the preheated oven for 45-55 minutes, or until the crust is golden brown and the filling is bubbly. You may need to cover the edges of the pie with aluminum foil during baking if they brown too quickly.
5. **Cool and Serve:**
   - Allow the pie to cool on a wire rack for at least 2 hours before serving. This allows the filling to set.
6. **Serve:**
   - Serve the pie warm or at room temperature, with a scoop of vanilla ice cream or a dollop of whipped cream if desired.

**Tips:**

- **Apple Varieties:** Use a mix of tart and sweet apples for the best flavor balance. Avoid using apples that are too soft, as they may turn mushy during baking.
- **Crust Handling:** Keep the dough as cold as possible to avoid a tough crust. If the dough becomes too warm, chill it briefly before rolling.
- **Thickening:** If you prefer a thicker filling, use cornstarch instead of flour. Adjust the amount based on your preference for filling consistency.

Enjoy your New York-style Apple Pie, a classic and comforting dessert that's perfect for any occasion!

www.ingramcontent.com/pod-product-compliance
Lightning Source LLC
LaVergne TN
LVHW081603060526
838201LV00054B/2045